OP 5.66

Dr. Agnes Lin
441 N. Oakhurst Dr. Suite 604
Beverly Hills, CA 90210

HEMINGWAY

a pictorial biography

HEMINGWAY

a pictorial biography

BY LEO LANIA

A STUDIO BOOK

THE VIKING PRESS · NEW YORK

Published in 1961 by The Viking Press, Inc.
625 Madison Avenue, New York 22, N.Y.

Published in German by Kindler Verlag, Munich
Translated by Joan Bradley
Library of Congress Catalog Card Number 61–8826
Printed in Germany

No OTHER AUTHOR of our time has had such a general and lasting influence on the generation which grew up between the world wars as Ernest Hemingway. Doubtless, the importance of James Joyce as the revolutionary pioneer of a new type of novel is greater; the effect of Franz Kafka and Thomas Mann, of T. S. Eliot and Dos Passos on contemporary literature penetrates deeper. Their subject matter and psychological insight moulded to a far greater extent the attitude to life of the western intellectual. Hemingway's influence, however, is not confined to literature and art, nor to the intellectual élite, nor even to one country. He is one of the most popular living authors among all classes of the reading public, young or old, both in the West and in the Communist countries.

No sooner was Hemingway's first novel *The Sun also Rises* published, than the youth of the 'twenties chose him as their example and ideal. Young American authors began to copy his style. Overnight, boys and girls at College and University spoke like his leading characters and assumed their way of life — their outward behaviour, melancholy nihilism, drinking and loving.

He also found a following in European literature and, not least, in modern journalism.

This influence was not always beneficial. The American literary critic Professor Philip Young writes that low literature, especially modern American detective novels, thrillers and gangster films, is 'full of Hemingway'; authors like Raymond Chandler, to name only one of the more successful, imitate Hemingway's writing, his impassive descriptions of brutality and crime. The drunks, neurotics, nymphomaniacs, drug addicts and homosexuals they present are modelled on characters from Hemingway's short stories and novels.

As Young explains, Hemingway has never considered force and crime an end in itself. His ruthless treatment of sexual crimes and errors has never been mere sensationalism or thirst for publicity. His imitators, however, took the Hemingway formula — a mixture of his curt pregnant dialogue and a lavish helping of murder and sex — and called the result modern realism, after which Hollywood and the popular magazines cashed in on the new 'art-form'. It would be unjust to hold Hemingway responsible for this clever but unscrupulous opportunism. Many serious and important authors have learnt from him; from his incorruptible objectivity, his exceptional gift of observation; from his language, as clear as the mountain stream which reveals each single pebble on the bottom. He has done more than anybody else to strip American literature of sentimentality and free American prose from bombast and artificial pathos. He has shown a complete generation of authors how to write natural and unliterary dialogue with a rhythm and authenticity which few other contemporary novelists have equalled.

Nevertheless, Hemingway's widespread popularity is not explained by the quality of his work or his literary talent alone. This is all the more remarkable when we recall that he has never belonged to any of the recognised modern literary schools.

In 1918 when the young men returning from the trenches screamed out their

Hemingway's films enrapture the masses: Humphrey Bogart (right), in *To Have and Have Not*, succumbs to the rich . . .

...and Spencer Tracy triumphs over the sea (discussing production with
Hemingway during the filming of *The Old Man and the Sea*)

horror and bitter despair at the mass murder of the war, Hemingway's voice
showed no sign of emotion. It was as though he were a neutral observer. While
the expressionists despised naturalism, damning all conformity, Hemingway's
only concern was the exact rendering of detail. In the age of expressionism he
was an impressionist, almost neo-classic in his precise presentation of detail, his
respect for form and discipline, his desire for perfection, the exact phrase, the
right word. He was nearer to the great naturalists of the nineteenth century than
to the 'storm and stress' writers of the twentieth.

During the early 'thirties social realism denied literature all independence
and demanded that it become a weapon in the fight for a new world constitu-

An admirer of bullfights, he has the theory
explained to him by Miguel Luis
Dominguin (left) – he studies the practice
frequently at the bullring (right)

tion. Hemingway withdrew, not to an ivory tower, but to Africa. He sought
his heroes, not among the champions and victims of the social revolution, but
among professional boxers, lion-hunters and bullfighters. How they survived
the tests of physical exertion and danger seemed to him of greater importance
than the problems of a class war.

Is this conscious renunciation of politics, the 'antisocial individualism' with
which many of his critics reproach him, an explanation for his successes and his
impact? Does it express the apathy of a generation tired of all politics? Does it
show their secret wish to flee from the drabness of everyday life, from themselves and all their troubles and fears; the wish to lose themselves in a colourful
and exotic world, surrounded by romance — even if this is the underworld of
gangsters?

If so, Hemingway's popularity in the Soviet Union would be double inex-
plicable. It would also be untrue to say that he completely shuts himself off
from the critical problems of our time. In truth, he is a rebel against our society,
a critic of our times, although his rebellion and criticism lie too deep for the
superficial reader who is only interested in the plot of a Hemingway story.

A key to understanding Hemingway can be found in the characters of his
heroes and in their beliefs. The leading character appears in various guises in
the different novels and short stories but basically he is always the same type.
Whether ordinary soldier or general, smuggler or gambler, Negro or journalist
— he is a man scarred by experience. He has always been gravely wounded,

Letters litter his table

physically or mentally, either during the war, in the sports arena, during his childhood, in the fight for existence. At some time or other something terrible has happened to him and the memory, often suppressed into the subconscious, persecutes him. However strong and tough he seems, he is fundamentally sick. He must prove himself to himself: his strength and his courage are nothing but a victory over fear. Maxwell Geismar describes the courage of Hemingway's heroes as the 'courage of despair'. It is as though, says Geismar, like men accused of crime in earlier ages, they seek to prove their innocence by showing that fire cannot destroy them.

Hemingway's principal character is almost always an American from the Middle West. He is no intellectual but his primitiveness is only a mask for his sensitivity. In order to master life he needs a moral code he can follow, a belief in certain rules by which to measure his behaviour. Neither books, reason nor religion can supply him with this belief. He needs the practical experience and example of men who live and die by these rules — the soldier, the bullfighter, and even the gangster.

Hemingway's world is a world at war — war either in the literal sense or the ruthless, brutal fight for existence. A hostile, unsympathetic world. Those who wish to survive must know how to kill.

In his short stories Hemingway sums up his philosophy of life in one sentence: 'A man can be destroyed but not defeated.' The speaker is an old bullfighter who although overcome, does not surrender and therefore proves the victor. In another story a champion boxer provides a similar example. In his latest work, *The Old Man and the Sea,* the old Cuban fisherman triumphs through the fanatical tenacity of his fight with the great fish, although in the end the sharks eat away his prey and so deprive him of the reward for his indescribable exertion and sacrifice.

This theme runs like a continuous thread through all of Hemingway's works. His outlook may be limited and incomplete, his conception of honour and heroes primitive, even childish; but this very limitation and primitiveness were bound to find a powerful response among a generation which expected its salvation from men of strength and uncorrupted instinct, since reason and knowledge had not averted the catastrophe, and which, in protest against the failure of its elders, proclaimed its own immaturity and lack of education and experience as virtues, and as the promise of a better future.

Just as caricatures often expose more of a man's character than the most faithful portrait, Hemingway's imitators reveal certain intellectual and emotional elements in his work which are typical of our time: the glorification of strength,

As leading reporter in the Spanish Civil War – and as champion angler in Idaho

infantile amorality, preoccupation with sex, anti-intellectualism. As Professor Carlos Baker, one of Hemingway's biographers, has remarked: 'The great philosopher, Henry Bergson, advised his students to think like men of action and act like men of thought. Hemingway has simplified this principle. His characters act as though thought were unthinkable.'

The part played by women in Hemingway's work is significant. That he handles sex without sentimentality and prudishness only strict moralists would hold against him. This was not only part of his poetic licence but also an important

The hunter at home – many trophies
hang on the walls

contribution to our knowledge of ourselves. But Hemingway not only knocked
Eros from his pedestal, he degraded him at the same time to a brutal and
cowardly procurer. Even the most important apostles and proclaimers of sensual
love, for instance D. H. Lawrence, discern in it the fulfilment of more than
a physical urge. They see it as the mystical desire of man and woman for a more
complete and satisfying union, whereas Hemingway's lovers have nothing in
common either spiritually or intellectually, nor do they seek it. They are not
partners — not even enemies. Their relationship is therefore neither exalted
nor tragic, it is not even a mutual adventure. It has always a flavour of rape
or the brothel.

A great shot! Hunting buffalo is
Hemingway's particular passion

The heroine is either a 'man-eater', a disturbing, even dangerous, element in
a man's world — *Men Without Women* was the characteristic title of one of his
short story anthologies — or a passive creature, completely subservient to man,
a willing instrument in the satisfaction of his desire. It is not surprising therefore that his women seem unreal, like the stereotypes you find on the front
pages of popular magazines, or the ideal women in the dreams of College students.

The bed or the sleeping bag is just as much a proving ground of the true man
as the sports arena or the battlefield. Hard and aggressive, he proves his virility exclusively by his sexual potency.

If this idea — characteristic though it may be — were the true essence of his work, and if the elements mentioned constituted the whole of it, then in spite of his great literary talent, Hemingway could not occupy the place he has won for himself in contemporary world literature, a place which earned him the Nobel Prize. He just cannot be classed with his numerous imitators. He is a poet, and behind his portrayals of character, his factual reports, and his fiction there is the beat of a suffering heart and the agonised wrestling of a wounded soul — the heart and soul of Hemingway himself.

The autobiographical nature of Hemingway's novels and stories provides the key to their true meaning. The hero of a Hemingway novel is Hemingway. His life unfolds the secret and explains the paradox in his art. It is important, since Hemingway reacts as sensitively as a seismograph to all the variations and shocks of our age; it is illuminating, since Hemingway's whole life consists of a striving towards truth. He once remarked that a writer's mission is to tell the truth. The determination with which he strips every last falsehood, every conventional hypocrisy from the very innermost recesses of human existence, his unconditional refusal to compromise, these constitute the most thrilling adventure in a life packed with adventure.

No aesthetic research into or analysis of his creations can say so much about them or their creator as the story of his life.

Ernest Hemingway was born on 21st July, 1899, in Oak Park, a small town in the state of Illinois. It is a community of prosperous citizens who look down with a certain amount of arrogance on the nearby 'proletarian', immoral and corrupt town of Chicago. 'The wonder to me,' said one of Hemingway's teachers, 'is how a boy brought up in Christian and Puritan nurture, should know and write so well of the devil and the underworld.'

Hemingway's family were prominent members of Oak Park society. His

Oak Park, Illinois, June 24, 1911

DR. CLARENCE E. HEMINGWAY
Newly Elected President of the Auxplaines
Medical Society.

Dr Clarence E. Hemingway, the author's father, a distinguished citizen of Oak Park

Ernest and his sister, Marcelline, in the Oak Park High School yearly report. They devoted their free time to sport, numerous clubs and the school magazine, *Trapeze*

father, Clarence Edmonds Hemingway, was a busy doctor, a dedicated hunter and fisherman, prouder of the pheasant and deer he shot with skill than of the patients he snatched from death. His mother, Grace, née Hall — her family, also, belonged to 'high society' — had entirely different interests: religion and music. She sang in the church choir and named her daughters after saints. She also insisted that Ernest, the second of her six children and her eldest son, should study music from his earliest childhood. She bought him a 'cello and personally supervised his daily practising. However, his father gave him a fishing rod for his third birthday, and at the age of ten Ernest was already the proud possessor of a gun. The woods and streams of the surrounding countryside had a far greater attraction for him than the music room. He did not become a 'cellist and was not at all interested in the church choir.

Family life was not without its tensions. Years later Hemingway was to re-

ERNEST HEMINGWAY

Class Prophet; Orchestra (1) (2) (3); Trapeze Staff (3), Editor (4); Class Play; Burke Club (3) (4); Athletic Association (1) (2) (4); Boys' High School Club (3) (4); Hanna Club (1) (3) (4); Boys' Rifle Club (1) (2) (3); Major Football (4); Minor Football (2) (3); Track Manager (4); Swimming (4).

"None are to be found more clever than Ernie."

ILLINOIS

MARCELLINE HEMINGWAY

Commencement Speaker; Orchestra (1) (2) (3) (4); Glee Club (3) (4); Tabula Board (4); Trapeze Staff (3), Editor (4); Opera (1) (2) (3); Atalanta (1) (2) (3) (4); Girls' Rifle Club (2) (3) (4); Commercial Club (4); Drama Club (3) (4); Girls' Club (3), Council (4); Story Club (3).

"I'd give a dollar for one of your dimples, Marc."

OBERLIN

Club ontest.

her

4).

that

mark that the best schooling for a writer was an unhappy childhood. One cannot say that his own childhood was unhappy, although the latent battle between his father, who wanted to make a 'proper man' of Ernest, and his mother, who wished to pass on her enthusiasm for the arts to her son, must have left its mark on the boy's development. Ernest had all the physical attributes to fulfil the hopes of his father, but he was also sensitive. The influence of his father was greater than that of his mother. Nevertheless, one realises from his early short stories in which he tells of the adventures and feelings of Nick, that his relationship with his father was not entirely without complications. Many years later Dr Clarence Edmonds Hemingway committed suicide. In the novel *For Whom the Bell Tolls* the hero, Jordan, touches on the subject of his father's suicide and says: 'I'll never forget how sick it made me the first time I knew he was a . . . coward.' And Jordan continues: 'If he wasn't a coward he would have

Hemingway's school: Oak Park High School

stood up to that woman and had not let her bully him. I wonder what I would have been like if he had married a different woman.'

This paragraph in the novel, although undoubtedly reflecting a personal experience, must not lead us to regard Ernest's childhood in a dark or even tragic light. He may have had his fits of depression and bitterness, as do most sensitive youngsters, but his robustness, his practical mind and above all his ambition always helped him over such periods. He wished to distinguish himself, always to be first — on the sports ground as well as in the classroom — and he was successful. There was no time for brooding and introspection.

He was not satisfied with school or with his way of life. Twice he ran away from home, but each time he soon returned to the safety and warmth of the family hearth. He was a rebellious and adventurous child but never difficult or

The form committee: Ernest in the centre

THE TRAPEZE

Our Motto:
The Best Is None Too
Good for Us.

OAK PARK, ILL., FRIDAY, APRIL 20, 1917.

PRICE 2 CENTS

REAL SERVICE

OAK PARK SECOND IN NORTHWESTERN U

CULVER TAKES MEET

By Ernest Hemingway

Individual prowess by Clarence Savage, Jack Lockyer and Walter Blount brought Oak Park 24½ points in the Northwestern U. National Interscholastic and the work of the medley relay team which placed second added enough points to give the Orange and Blue team second place. They shared second honors with Cicero and La Grange, each team amassing 12½ points.

Culver Military Academy, with a well balanced team took the meet with a total of 37 points.

Savage was Oak Park's individual star, gathering a second in both the high and low hurdles. Lockyer placed second in the dash only a hair's breadth behind Dowling of Bowen. Blount, who was doped to win the 660 yard run, was forced to start at the very end of a squad of about twenty runners but succeeded in passing all but two of them.

Oak Park's medley relay team, composed of Lockyer, King, Moore and Sutphen, ran an excellent race and copped second place. The medley team would have won handily but for the fact that Weston Moore was unable to put up his usual fine race, due to an injury to his leg, which was hurt when he was tripped and had a bad spill in the qualifying heats Friday night.

Oak Park's indoor track team this season was handicapped ever since the first race by inability to put its full strength in the field due to the absence in the last two meets of Captain Pentecost due to sickness and the ineligibility of star athletes all during the season.

Prospects for an out door track championship are very brilliant as Pentecost is again out and the other missing athletes have made up their scholastic deficiencies. With all their talent out Oak Park will have the best team in the Suburban League.

The track at the new field is in fine shape and it is very probable the Suburban outdoor interscholastic will be held here.

In the Beloit meet on May 5th, Oak Park will enter a team and also in the Lake Forest interscholastic, May 12, and the big Illinois interscholastic, May 19.

GIRLS CLUB HOLDS FINAL MEETING

Entire Year Has Been Successful—Girls Have Heard Good Programs

MISS BARTELME LAST SPEAKER

By Helen Carr

Girls' club assembled last Wednesday afternoon to hear Miss Mary Bartelme, assistant to Judge Arnold of the juvenile court of Chicago. An unusually large audience came out to this last meeting of the year to hear the climax of a year's good programs.

Miss Bartelme thanked the girls for the spirit of sympathy and helpfulness which has expressed itself in action more than in words, since she last spoke in Oak Park. She mentioned especially the appreciation of the young girls who were sent across the lake last summer for a vacation, by funds given from Oak Park. To those who, living in Chicago, had never seen the lake, others whose greatest travel had been a street car ride, and the majority who had never seen three square meals appear on their home tables in succession, this experience was a wonderfully happy one.

These girls have never forgotten this great event in their lives and wonder if they will ever have anything like again.

The girls whose homes, for one reason or another, are unfit for them to remain there unless she can bring home five dollars a week, a pretty little Greek girl deserted by her mother, tiny girls who have tried to die before anything worse could happen, are fair samples of those brought to the home, to remain there temporarily, until homes can be found for them. But they forget the hard times under the kindly care of Miss Fritz, and the helpful interest of Miss Bartelme. Miss Fritz is the head of the home and in her Miss Bartelme is finding a willing aid in bringing these girls the kind of a life they should have. The home is in a neighborhood where they see a great many automobiles, and the children often sigh for a ride. Any one who would like to give it to them would be most welcome.

Other aids mentioned by Miss Bartelme can be given to her through Miss Rattray and Miss Chamberlain.

PROM PLANS TO PROCEED

Seniors and Juniors Vote to Continue Work on Prom.

By Elwood Ratcliff

On account of the uncertain conditions into which the country has been thrown by being forced into war, there was some doubt in the minds of many parents, whether or not it would be better to give up the Junior

GIRLS' CONFERENCE THIS WEEK END

Inspiring Program Laid Out—Miss Ruth Tapping, Miss Grogan and Mr. Dixondorfer, Speakers.

GIRLS FROM 15 TO 19 ADMITTED

By Marcelline Hemingway

The most inspiring series of meetings ever held in Oak Park is to take place this week end under the name

Ernest, the academician.
In the school magazine he
enlarged upon the advantages
of a practical, rather than
a theoretical education

neurotic. Otherwise he would not have been the excellent scholar he was — 'top of his form' as the school yearly report confirms, — nor would he have been so popular amongst his comrades.

These friends respected and admired him particularly for his sporting achievements. He started boxing lessons at the age of fourteen. In the very first hour of his instruction a blow from his professional opponent shattered his nose and a few weeks later he received an eye injury which permanently damaged his sight. In spite of this he finished the course.

These were the first of many injuries he was to receive during the course of his life. During his years at High School he had to be carried off the football field twice. As someone once said to Gertrude Stein, who discovered him and became his literary mentor: as soon as Ernest tried a new sport he broke something — an arm, a leg or his skull. Apart from the serious injuries he received

Ernest, the sportsman:

Among the swimmers
(front row,
second from the left)

Among the athletes
(in civilian clothes,
as manager)

Among the footballers
(front row,
second from the right)

THE TRAPEZE

A Weekly Newspaper Issued by the Publishing Board of the Oak Park and River Forest Township High School

Entered as second class matter Nov. 17, 1916, at the postoffice at Oak Park, Ill., under the Act of March 3, 1879.

BUSINESS STAFF

Business Manager..Gordon Shorney
Assistant   Wilbur Brandt
Advertising Manager..Dale Bumstead

Assistants

Wiley Caldwell   Julian Lull

Deskroom Agents

205 Grace Dabbert.   313 Clarence Savage.
211 Edward Willcox.   304 Harold Wright.
202 Wilbur Brandt.   102 Fred Brightly.
204 Elwood Ratcliff. 106 Irvin Houck.
209 Russel Warren.   108 Harold Kaiser.
301 Dixie Davis.   111 Lewis Murray.
303 Joseph Godfrey.   113 Roland Popkin.
305 Constance Long.   115 Helen Rogers.
307 Margaret Patch.   117 Gorin Smith.
210 Howard Vaughan   104 Parker Hamilton.
   207 Morris Musselman.

EDITORIAL STAFF

Editor .....Ernest Hemingway

Associate Editors

Earle Pashley   LeRoy Huxham
Susan Lowrey   Elliot Smeeth.
     Marcelline Hemingway.

Airline Pilot......Morris Musselman
Cartoonist..........Albert Dungan

Reporters

Arthur Thexton   Florence Winder
Allen Speelman   Edward Andresen
Laura Canode   Helen Sinclair
Fred Wilcoxen   Raymond George
Franklin Lee   Annabel Marchant
Helen Carr   Ray Ohlsen
Jack Pentecost   Clarence Savage

Faculty Advisors.

Business. ....Mr. Owen
Editorial ....Mr. Gehlman

WHAT THE TRAPEZE HAS ACCOMPLISHED

Several notable changes have been made this year in the Trapeze in a

es. T
crawle
trench
ing sp
trench
the ar
ran.
operat
artiller
dropp
their
shells
wea'-
enemic
down
band
line tr
of so
"team
    Our
ignorir
of ou
You v
    Rem
—Oak

CL

SENIC

G

B

Ther
everybe
they d
say? S
very
right.
This
give th
progra
School
Of c
history
course
think)
cause
woman
ish anc
credulc
Virgi
ful poe
day an
perings
Fritz

Editor:
Ernest Hemingway

during the First World War on the Italian front — on that occasion 227 steel splinters had to be removed from his right leg — Hemingway has, the statistics tell us, survived shot wounds in both feet, both knees and both hands and also six severe head injuries. He has been involved in three car crashes, one of which (in London during the Second World War) necessitated 57 stitches. In 1946 he broke six ribs, and he himself puts the number of times he has had concussion at at least ten. His body is covered in scars. Or is it only his body?

His great interest in literature was already noticeable at Oak Park High School. It was cultivated by two of his teachers who recognised his literary talent in its early stages. He edited the school magazine, regularly writing contributions himself, including a 'gossip column', harmless and often witty chatter about the doings of his friends.

He wrote poems and short stories, less remarkable for their originality or

In the footsteps of Ring Lardner

A "RING LARDNER" ON THE BLOOMINGTON GAME

Right half Smearcase of Bloomington kicked off to Cole who returned the ball to his own one-yard line. Wilcoxen signalled for the hit and run play but Gordon was caught at second by a perfect throw from the catcher. Hemingway went over for the first touchdown by way of the Lake Street 'L.' Colville missed goal, the ball hitting the bar and causing havoc with the free lunch.
Score, Oak Park 6, Bloomington 0.
Wilkins replaced Cole. Blum kicked off to fullback Roquefort of Bloomington, who was nailed in his tracks. Baldwin of Oak Park wielded the hammer. On the first ball pitched Limburger cracked one to Moore, who stepped on the bag and shot to Wilcoxen at first, doubling the runner.
Savage tried a drop kick from the 90-yard line but it went foul by three inches. Timme then smashed through center for 110 yards for Oak Park's touchdown. Thistlewaite kicked goal.
Score, Oak Park 13, Bloomington 0.
Time was called but refused to answer.

Second Quarter
Lofberg went in at Worthington's tackle. Kendall kicked off to Eycleshymer's front porch. Ball was run back by Quarterback Cambrian to Oak Park's line of demarcation. Thistlewaite on incomplete returns claimed three precincts out of 1,396. Hemingway made a tackle. Miss Biggs fainted. Thistlewaite was carried unconscious from the field. Time was called while Fat Tod sent out for a package of censored * Maker's name furnished on request.
Dunning kicked out of Danger and Lofberg shot a basket from the middle of the field.

Score, Oak Park 15, Bloomington 0.
The captains matched pennies to see who would kick off. Shepherd lost and Bloomington kicked to Phelps, who knocked a clean three-bagger, scoring Bell, George and Golder. Hill popped to the pitcher.
Score, Oak Park 18, Bloomington 0.
Wilcoxen went color blind and tackled the water boy. Canode went in at Fullback. The lightning fast Hemingway scored Oak Park's third touchdown, crossing the goal line by way of the Chicago avenue car line, transferring at Harlem and Lake.
Thexton missed goal, the ball striking the bar and falling to the brass rail.
Score, Oak Park 24, Bloomington 0.
Overstreet kicked the ball outside the field and was penalized twenty-seven yards for unnecessary roughness. Wilcoxen again went color blind and tackled a goal post. He was penalized thirty-eight yards for holding.
"Dope" MacNamara replaced the slight Wilkins, who was injured by a kick in the middle of the line of scrimmage.
The game broke up in a riot when the student Cops refused to keep the crowd off the field unless they were given Major Monograms as a farther incentive.
Final score:
Oak Park 24, Bloomington 0.

Late Bulletin
Hemingway is reported as convalescing, but the Doctors Fear his mind is irreparably Lost.

Later
A large and enthusiastic crowd attended Hemingway's Funeral. A pleasant Time was had By all.

PERSONALS
By LeRoy Huxham.
William Johnstone, '16, was rushed for the Sigma Alpha Phi.

Paul Tubilock attended Grand Opera last Saturday night.

Agnes Hecox and Mary Gallagher have taken up charity work.

The janitors are to be thanked for the briliance of our athletic trophies.

Mr. Erickson is anxious to have a few more tenors in the Glee club.

Warre Boden led Christian Endeavor at the Harvard church last Sunday.

About eighty Seniors will attend Henry VII. at the Illinois, Wednesday evening.

Tom Linnell, '15, has been elected treasurer of the sophomore class at Lake Forest.

Stuart Standish remarked that Mr. Platt and Mr. Lofberg happened on the same sale of neckties.

Elizabeth Duffield and Hazel Reading led the meeting of the Y. P. U. last Sunday at the Second Congregational church.

Edward Ohlsen and David Colville attempted with little success to purchase two sundaes for 11 cents at a one-cent sae in La Porte.

Helen Shepherd and Bessie Yager upheld the affirmative and Francis Bumstead and Marcelline Hemingway, the negative of a debate at Plymouth club last Sunday.

Florence Toutelot, Annette De Voe, Katherine Meyers, Al Dungan visited U. of I. last Saturday, where they enjoyed the football game and the dance.

Helen Cribben, a sophomore, who has been out of school so far this year with eye trouble, visited Indian-

SWIMMING TEAM ROUNDING | MINOR BASKETBALL TEAM

Class Prophecy

Ernest Hemingway, '17

"GO over to that table and take the news as it comes from the front," said General Wilcoxen to me. I seated myself at the radio table in the headquarters and adjusted the phones to my ears. Clickety, click, click, click, click, click went the receivers.

"Read it off to me as it comes in," said General Wilcoxen, and I read off the messages as rapidly as possible.

"Dale Bumstead, great powder magnate, captured and held for ransom by the Germans. Shall we pay the $2,000,000 asked for his return?"

"Don't ask foolish questions," snapped the general.

"General Taylor, Major Swanson and Colonel Rawls have been recommended to command the new expeditionary force. Have you any choice which is the best?"

"Say there is no choice," growled the commander-in-chief.

"There's a man from outside that wants to take some pictures," said a sentry, saluting as he ushered in a familiar looking figure.

"Why, Tom Hildebrand, go as far as you like," said the general, and Tom immediately departed to send a wire to his wife, Ruth Bramberg, who had him report every night what he had done during the day.

The radio clicked again and I wrote down the message for the general. "The following Red Cross nurses have been recommended for the cross of exceptional bravery: Edna Hildman, Ina Peterson, Helen Sinclair and Mabel Tate."

"That's wonderful," said the general. "Give 'em each the double cross."

A loud noise and commotion started outside, and I hastened to the door. "Let me come in and see him. I know him. He'll be glad to see me. Let me in."

I reached the door in time to see the sleuth with his bayonet pressed against the rotund stomach of Mr. Le Roy Huxham, the Rip Van Winkle of the class.

"Hux, of all people! What have you been doing with yourself?" gasped Fred.

"Oh, nothing. Just dropped in to see you, old top."

"Sit down, old man, and tell us the news." Knowing Hux, I lay down on a camp cot, prepared for a long session.

"Well," he began, "out of our old bunch of '17, had you heard about Dick and Henry Bredfield fighting a duel over Florence Winder? They both were shot, and Flossie died of a broken heart. You heard about the big war time athletic benefit, didn't you? Pete Chase won the back stroke, Grimm the quarter mile, and Preucil the national tennis title.

"You remember Jack Lander, don't you? Well, old Jasper has started a new religion called Jazzism, and Peaslee and Art Thexton are his favorite disciples. His cult is the

Hemingway as 'class prophet' in the school yearly report

imagination than for the proof they provided of his gift for precise observation. He took his themes from the social sphere he had just started to explore and which particularly fascinated him — the world of the champion boxers whom he had encountered in the sports club in Chicago. The stories were pregnant and terse, they were made to develop correctly — with a beginning, a middle and an end, — free from the lyrical and personal digressions so characteristic of the literary effusions of any ordinary sixteen-year-old. His poetry clearly betrayed the influence of Kipling. He adopted the rhythm of Kipling's ballads and attempted to copy their verve, their unsentimental hardness and virility.

In April 1917, America entered the war. Ernest Hemingway was preparing for his matriculation. He wanted to volunteer for military service immediately, but his father would not hear of it. 'Ernest is too young,' he decided and would brook no further discussion. However, the boy fought so stubbornly when both his parents tried to persuade him to continue his studies at College that they were forced to give in. Hemingway is the only representative American author who has never been to a University.

He was no longer satisfied with life at home. He wanted to stand on his own feet and try his luck in the world. His father's younger brother lived in Kansas City where he was a successful merchant and a close friend of the editor of the 'Star', the local newspaper. It was decided that Ernest should depart for Kansas City. His uncle promised to get him a job as reporter on the 'Star', at that time among the six best American papers.

The seven months he spent on the staff of the 'Star' were of the utmost importance to Hemingway. Journalism and war — these had the greatest effect on his literary development. They moulded and decided his style, his art, his whole life.

Hemingway has often emphasised how valuable a training was his apprenticeship with the paper. Unlike other large newspapers, the 'Star' was not obsessed with the need for famous names; indeed the assistant-editor for local news, Hemingway's immediate superior, C. G. Wellington, took a pride in forming his staff from young, inexperienced men who showed journalistic talent. They had to work hard and above all learn the style which had made the paper famous throughout America. Each new reporter received a list of basic rules to be followed in all his articles and reports. The first of these read: Use short sentences. The first sentence must be short. Acquire a pithy style. Be positive, never negative! Unnecessary adjectives fell victim to the red pencil. Hemingway once mentioned that in the 'Star' you must never write that someone had been seriously injured — all injuries were serious. The wound had to be described as superficial or dangerous. Bombast, clichés and the flowery phrases so popular with American newspapers of that time were forbidden.

During his time with the 'Star', Hemingway acquired a clear and simple style and learnt to handle the English language like an instrument that only one who practises for hours daily can master. But that was not all; as a local reporter he had came into direct contact with reality. The events he had to report could not be calmly reasoned out at a writing-table, there was no choice of plot, be it in a case of murder, accident or fire. He had to be on the spot, learn to see everything with his own eyes; no gift of invention or imagination could take the place of immediate personal experience. Many of his reports for the 'Star', often only a few sentences in length, later became subjects for the stories which made him famous.

Hemingway's first war experience: the collapse of the front and the Italian retreat.
On the right: The firing of an Austrian mortar in the Italian theatre of war

His activity as a reporter was stimulating and educational but it did not satisfy the restless, energetic Hemingway. He wanted to go to war. Twice he had volunteered and each time been turned down because of his bad eye. One of his colleagues on the 'Star', with whom he had struck up a close friendship, had recently returned from the European theatre of war where, although completely blind in one eye, he had served as a driver of an American ambulance at the French front. In April 1918 both of them heard that the Red Cross needed fresh volunteers for the Italian army. They decided to report immediately. On 12th May they received their uniforms in New York and shortly afterwards embarked for Europe.

Hemingway was assigned to a field ambulance serving behind the Piave front. He was full of enthusiasm. He wrote to his friends on the 'Star' that he was having a splendid time. Here was the great adventure, the experience he had thirsted for all these years. The only complaint which recurred in his letters to his friends at home was that nothing happened in his sector. In front of the billets, a deserted mill, there was a large field where he and the other drivers played baseball. They swam in the near-by stream and sunbathed. The front was only a few miles distant, but the peacefulness was only disturbed by the daily shooting practice of the various batteries. Boring.

Hemingway decided to transfer to a different division of the Medical Corps or to a different troop, in order 'to find out where the war was really going on'.

His wish was quickly fulfilled. The front began to move as the Italian counter-offensive got under way. He reported to one of the Red Cross canteens which had been put up behind the trenches. His predecessor, an American lieutenant, had fallen here shortly before. Hemingway, however, was still not satisfied. He persuaded the sector commander to allow him to take parcels into the trenches

Biographical episodes on the screen:
Hemingway's experiences at the front in the first film version
of the novel *A Farewell to Arms*

themselves. From then on he penetrated daily to the foremost positions — a most welcome guest to the soldiers, providing them with cigars, cigarettes and chocolates.

A week later, at the beginning of July 1918, two weeks before his nineteenth birthday, these expeditions came to a sudden end near the village of Fossalta. A grenade from a trench mortar landed a few feet from Hemingway. The Italian soldier whose coffee he was pouring out was killed outright, another had his legs torn off and a third was gravely wounded. So was Hemingway. He lost consciousness. When he came to, he took his screaming comrade on his back and dragged himself away. An enemy searchlight picked him out, and after a few steps he stumbled into the scattered fire of a machine-gun. He collapsed, hit several times. 'My feet', he later wrote to his family, 'felt like I had rubber boots full of water (hot water) and my knee cap was acting queer. The machine-gun bullet just felt like a sharp smack on the leg with an icy snowball.' He again lost consciousness and regained it only when he was on a stretcher. His comrade was dead.

Hemingway was carried to the medical centre two miles away. The battle was now in full swing and the route was under constant fire. Time and time again the stretcher-bearers had to desert their burden and take cover.

Hemingway spent five days in the field hospital. Twenty-eight steel splinters were removed from his leg before he was declared fit to be moved and admitted to a hospital in Milan. There he lay for three months, undergoing no less than twelve operations.

In his letters to his parents he promised that after his recovery he would remain with the rest of the Medical Corps at a respectful distance from the front. Nevertheless, on his discharge from hospital in the autumn he volunteered for the Italian infantry. During the two months until the armistice, when the

Hemingway in
the Milan hospital
(1918)

Love in the shadow of war: film versions of two Hemingway novels (left, *A Farewell to Arms*, right, *The Sun also Rises*)

fighting along the Italian front was at its most bitter, he fought in the field.

At the end of the war Hemingway was a lieutenant, proud possessor of the War Service Cross, of the second highest Italian honour, the Silver Medal for Gallantry, and an aluminium knee-cap.

After his release, he returned to America in January 1919. His nerves were shattered. He suffered from insomnia and was tortured by nightmares; he was afraid of the dark and for months a night-light burned in his room. He was unable to banish his memories of the war. He attempted to purge his mind of these recollections by writing about his experiences in many of his stories and best novels.

Hemingway's attitude towards war has remained inconsistent throughout his life. On the one hand he registers with surprising sincerity his horror of war, never making it sound wonderful or glorious, on the other hand he never raises any complaint or protest against it. It is his belief that the horrors of war are unavoidable and all that a man can do is to pass the test with dignity and courage. Fifteen years later he explained to a young writer the first thing that

an author should take to heart: 'As a man things are as they should or shouldn't
be. As a man you know who is right and who is wrong. You have to make
decisions and enforce them. As a writer you should not judge. You should understand.'

To understand all is to forgive all, says the French proverb. However, it is
not easy to be that wise at the age of twenty. While so many soldiers returned
from the front as rebels and other wallowed in self-pity, at odds with the world
and themselves, Hemingway sank into a state of disillusioned nihilism. One day
he confessed to an old friend that he was in love — but he described his relations
with the opposite sex as a great but passing happiness.

The township of Oak Park, his parents' house, his old friends — he was no
longer in tune with his former life. He had to get away.

Hemingway had a clear picture of his ambition: to be an author and write
the 'great American novel'. He intended to get work with another newspaper
to earn his living; in his free time he would concentrate on writing. He was
confident that in a short time he would be able to live from his books.

In July he followed his parents to Michigan where the family owned a summer house by the lake. He remained there when the rest of the family returned
to Oak Park in the autumn. His time was spent fishing, reading and writing.
He wrote dozens of stories, tirelessly sending them to magazines and having
them returned with monotonous regularity.

One of the family's friends, also spending the summer in Michigan, was a
successful business man in Toronto, Canada. He took a great liking to Dr
Hemingway's eldest son and recommended him to the editor of the 'Toronto Star
Weekly'. This periodical was not a newspaper, but printed features and short
stories of entertainment value. At Kansas City Hemingway had achieved
perfection as a reporter; in Toronto he had the opportunity to try his hand

March 6, 1920.

TAKING A CHANCE FOR A FREE SHAVE

Submitting Your Face to Beginners at Barber College Calls for Grit.

TO BARGAIN-CHASERS

You May Have Twenty-Five Teeth Extracted for $2 at Dental College.

By ERNEST M. HEMINGWAY.

THE land of the free and the home of the brave is the modest phrase used by certain citizens of the republic to the south of us to designate the country they live in. They may be brave—but there is nothing free. Free lunch passed some time ago and on attempting to join the Free Masons you are informed that it will cost you seventy-five dollars.

The true home of the free and the brave is the barber college. Everything is free there. And you have to be brave. If you want to save $5.60 a month on shaves and hair cuts go to the barber college, but take your courage with you.

For a visit to the barber college requires the cold, naked, valor of the man who walks clear-eyed to death. If you don't believe it, go to the beginner's department of the barber's college and offer yourself for a free shave. I did.

As you enter the building you come into a well-appointed barber shop on the main floor. This is where the students who will soon graduate work. Shaves cost five cents, haircuts fifteen.

"Next," called one of the students. The others looked expectant.

"I'm sorry," I said, "I'm going upstairs."

Upstairs is where the free work is done by the beginners.

A hush fell over the shop. The young barbers looked at one another significantly. One made an expressive gesture with his forefinger across his throat.

"He's going upstairs," said a barber in a hushed voice.

"He's going upstairs!" the other echoed him and looked at one another.

I went upstairs.

Here's Another One

UPSTAIRS there was a crowd of young fellows standing around in white jackets and a line of chairs ran down the wall. As I entered the room two or three went over and stood by their chairs. The others remained where they were.

"Come on you fellows, here's another one," called one of the white

Chicago: Hemingway's flight to Europe began here

as a feature writer. His contributions found favour and for the first time
he saw his name in print. His articles, often tinged with satire – whether they
dealt with the exposure of the war profiteers or the snobbery of certain circles
in Toronto society, – were good journalism. His income, though, was less than
modest. Ten dollars was the highest fee he received, but in the course of four
months fifteen of his contributions appeared and he considered himself a full-
time writer. He was, at the time, twenty-one years of age.

In the autumn of 1920 Hemingway took his leave of Toronto. He had spent
eight months there. Restlessness drove him on. He moved to Chicago.

Difficult weeks and months followed. He was often without a cent to his
name. He was able to share a furnished room with a war-time colleague, other
friends kept him from starving. He refused to admit defeat, however, and with-

Mark Twain (top left), Henry James (right), William Butler Yeats (below),
whose books Hemingway would rather read
than earn a million dollars a year

stood the temptation to return to the fleshpots of Oak Park. Now and then one
of his articles was accepted. As a temporary measure he acted as crime reporter
on the 'Chicago Tribune,' until he found a job with a monthly magazine which
was published by a financier as an advertisement for his speculations and invest-
ments. The experience Hemingway gained during this period of employment
was not calculated to increase the respect or sympathy he felt for peace-time
America. His employer was unscrupulous, a swindler who squeezed dry any
small or large speculator hopeful of a quick and fabulous profit. However, the
work earned Hemingway fifty dollars a week and left him enough free time for
his literary work.

A prosperous friend who had rented a large and elegant apartment from a
patroness of the arts, she having gone on a lengthy tour of Europe, immediately
put the vacant rooms at the disposal of his friends, among them Hemingway.

The group living there comprised the generous host, who occupied an important position in an advertising agency, his wife, his wife's younger sister, later
to marry the writer Don Passos, a friend of hers and two young men. They all
had literary ambitions. In this small writers' colony Hemingway was the
youngest, but, as his friends of that time were later to recall, also the most
diligent. While the others spent hours debating the nature and aims of modern
literature, Hemingway stayed in his room and wrote. While they developed
their theories on art, Hemingway turned a deaf ear to art and artists. Only
one question interested him: was the story he was occupied with at the moment
saleable? Did his latest poem stand a chance of being published?

His artistic principles were simple: authenticity, simplicity, directness. He
searched for them in literature, in painting and in music. During their evenings
of literary discussion he kept telling his friends that the reader must be able to
see, feel, smell and hear what the writer was trying to express.

Such evenings took on a special atmosphere of dedication when Sherwood Anderson visited them. His *Winesberg (Ohio)*, a collection of short stories, was one of the most successful books of the period. It served as a model for a whole generation of writers and was the foundation of the 'Chicago school' in modern American literature. Sherwood Anderson had a decisive influence on Hemingway, so decisive that many critics later declared that Hemingway had consciously copied and adopted his style and subject matter, but Anderson denied this allegation in his own memoirs. 'Hemingway's talent was his own and in no way influenced by me,' he wrote. This recognition is all the more remarkable since, in the meantime, Hemingway had shown his gratitude for Anderson's friendship and help by writing a novel in which Anderson and his works were the objects of satire.

This attack was the outcome of Hemingway's intolerance of any writer who did not share his literary ideas and concepts. Whoever refused to accept these without reservation was his bitter enemy. The break with Anderson was not

Sherwood Anderson helped to start Hemingway on his literary career

William Faulkner, who received the Nobel Prize for Literature five years before Hemingway

the only one of its kind. In later years a whole succession of writers, originally
Hemingway's patrons and friends, incurred the same treatment. He would not
allow his artistic principles to be attacked. Criticism he allowed, contradiction
he did not.

Every month he spent working on the financier's periodical added to his
disgust with the practices of his 'boss' in particular and with the provincial
Philistine atmosphere of Chicago in general. Hadley Richardson, a young girl
he had met in Michigan during the previous summer, had appeared in Chicago.
She was a singularly gifted pianist and soon became a permanent member of
the artistic circle. They were married in September 1921.

This was the era of prohibition, crass materialism, puritanical hypocrisy.
Gangsters and marathon dancers were the heroes of the day. Hadley was as
disgusted with America as was Ernest. Sherwood Anderson had just returned
from his first visit to Paris and his description of the free life, the artistic atmosphere and inspiration that awaited writers there, awakened in both young
people the desire to travel to Europe. As a result of the devaluation of the franc
one could live in Paris on even the most modest of dollar incomes. This was the
deciding factor.

The young couple journeyed first to Toronto, where Hemingway persuaded
the editor of the 'Star' to employ him as European correspondent. He was not
to draw a set salary, but each accepted contribution would be paid for in accord-
ance with the regular scale of fees. In addition, the paper would pay all expenses. Hemingway was entirely free to choose his own subjects and was not
tied to any particular place. His field of activity covered the whole of Europe.
This was an alluring offer for any twenty-two-year-old.

In December 1921, the Hemingways sailed to France. In his pocket Ernest
had numerous letters of introduction which Sherwood Anderson had addressed

MAGAZINE SECTION PART TWO
THE TORONTO STAR WEEKLY
MAGAZINE SECTION PART TWO

FOURTEENTH YEAR. TORONTO, SATURDAY, OCTOBER 20, 1923. 10c PER COPY

Bull Fighting Is Not a Sport—It Is a Tragedy

It Symbolizes the Struggle Between Man and Beasts—The Three Acts of the Drama Are the Entry, the Planting of Banderillos, and the Death of the Bull—a Canadian at Ringside.

By ERNEST M. HEMINGWAY

ENTRY OF THE CUADRILLAS

"WITH HIS MULETA THE TORERO MUST MAKE THE BULL MISS HIM AGAIN AND AGAIN BY INCHES, BEFORE HE IS ALLOWED TO KILL HIM."

"JUST AS THE BULL IS ABOUT TO HIT HIM THE BANDERILLERO DROPS THE DARTS INTO THE BULL'S HUMP JUST BACK OF THE HORNS"

IT was spring in Paris and everything looked just a little too beautiful. Mike and I decided to go to Spain. Strater drew us a fine map of Spain on the back of a menu of the Strix restaurant. On the same menu he wrote the name of a restaurant in Madrid where the specialty is young suckling pig roasted, the name of a pensione in the Via San Jeronima where the bull fighters live, and sketched a plan showing where the Grecos are hung in the Prado.

Fully equipped with this menu and our old clothes, we started for Spain. We had one objective—to see bull fights.

We left Paris one morning and got off the train at Madrid the next noon. We saw our first bull fight at 4.30 that afternoon. It took about two hours to get tickets. We finally got them from scalpers for twenty-five pesetas apiece. The bull ring was entirely sold out. We had barrera seats. These the scalper explained in Spanish and broken French were the first row of the ringside, directly under the royal box, and immediately opposite where the bull would come out.

We asked him if he didn't have any less distinguished seats for somewhere around twelve pesetas, but he was sold out. So we paid the fifty pesetas for the two tickets, and with the tickets in our pockets sat out on the sidewalk in front of a big cafe near the Puerto Del Sol. It was very exciting sitting out in front of a cafe your first day in Spain with a ticket in your pocket that meant that rain or shine you were going to see a bull fight in an hour and a half. In fact, it was so exciting that we started out for the bull ring on the outskirts of the city in about half an hour.

The bull ring or Plaza de Toros was a big, tawny brick amphitheatre standing at the end of a street in an open field. The yellow and red Spanish flag was floating over it. Carriages were driving up and people getting out of buses. There was a great crowd of beggars around the entrance. Men were selling water out of big terra cotta water bottles. Kids sold fans, canes, roasted salted almonds in paper spills, fruit and slabs of ice cream. The crowd was gay and cheerful but all intent on pushing toward the entrance. Mounted civil guards with patent leather cocked hats and carbines slung over their backs sat their horses like statues, and the crowd flowed through.

Inside they all stood around in the bull ring, talking and looking up in the grandstand at the girls in the boxes. Some of the men had field glasses in order to look better. We found our seats and the crowd began to leave the ring and get into the rows of concrete seats. The ring was circular—that sounds foolish, but a boxing ring is square—with a sand floor. Around it was a red board fence, just high enough for a man to be able to vault over it. Between the board fence, which is called the barrera, and the first row of seats ran a narrow alley way. Then came the seats which were just like a football stadium except that around the top ran a double circle of boxes.

EVERY seat in the amphitheatre was full. The arena was cleared. Then on the far side of the arena out of the crowd, four heralds in medieval costume stood up and blew a blast on their trumpets. The band crashed out, and from the entrance on the far side of the ring four horsemen in black velvet with ruffs around their necks rode out into the white glare of the arena. The people on the sunny side were baking in the heat and fanning themselves. The whole sol side was a flicker of fans.

Behind the four horsemen came the procession of the bull fighters. They had been all formed in ranks in the entrance way ready to march out, and as the music started they came. In the front rank walked the three espadas or toreros, who would have charge of the killing of the six bulls of the afternoon.

They came walking out in heavily brocaded yellow and black costumes, the familiar "toreador" suit, heavy with gold embroidery, cape, jacket, shirt and collar, knee breeches, pink stockings, and low pumps. Always at bull fights afterwards the incongruity of those pink stockings used to strike me. Just behind the three principals—and after your first bull fight you do not look at their costumes but their faces—marched the teams or cuadrillas. They are dressed in the same way but not as gorgeously as the matadors.

Back of the teams ride the picadors. Big, heavy, brown-faced men in wide flat hats, carrying lances like long window poles. They are astride horses that make Spark Plug look as trim and sleek as a King's Plate winner. Back of the pics come the gaily harnessed mule teams and the red-shirted monos or bull ring servants.

The bull fighters march in across the sand to the president's box. They march with easy professional stride, swinging along, not in the least theatrical except for their clothes. They all have the easy grace and slight slouch of the professional athlete. From their faces they might be major league ball players. They salute the president's box and then spread out along the barrera, exchanging their heavy brocaded capes for the fighting capes that have been laid along the red fence by the attendants.

We leaned forward over the barrera. Just below us the three matadors of the afternoon were leaning against the fence talking. One lighted a cigaret. He was a short, clear skinned gypsy, Gitanillo, in a wonderful gold brocaded jacket, his short pig-tail sticking out under his black cocked hat.

"He's not very fancy," a young man in a straw hat, with obviously American shoes, who sat on my left, said.

"But he sure knows bulls, that boy. He's a great killer."

"You're an American, aren't you?" asked Mike.

"Sure," the boy grinned. "But I know this gang. That's Gitanillo. You want to watch him. The kid with the chubby face is Chicuelo. They say he doesn't really like bull fighting, but the town's crazy about him. The one next to him is Villata. He's the great one."

I had noticed Villata. He was as straight as a lance and walked like a young wolf. He was talking and smiling at a friend who leaned over the barrera. Upon his tanned cheekbone was a big patch of gauze held on with adhesive tape.

"He got gored last week at Malaga," said the American.

The American, whom later we were to learn to know and love as the Gin Bottle King, because of a great feast of arms performed at an early hour of the morning with a container of Mr. Gordon's celebrated product as his sole weapon in one of the four most dangerous situations I have ever seen, said: "The show's going to begin."

OUT in the arena the picadors had galloped their decrepit horses around the ring, sitting straight and stiff in their rocking chair saddles. Now all but three had ridden out of the ring. These three were huddled against the red painted fence of the barrera. Their horses backed against the fence, one eye bandaged, their lances at rest.

In rode two of the marshals in the velvet jackets and white ruffs. They galloped up to the president's box, swerved and saluted, doffing their hats and bowing low. From the box an object came hurtling down. One of the marshals caught it in his plumed hat.

"The key to the bull pen," said the Gin Bottle King.

The two horsemen whirled and rode across the arena. One of them tossed the key to a man in torero costume, they both saluted with a wave of their plumed hats, and had gone from the ring. The big gate was shut and bolted. There was no more entrance. The ring was complete.

The crowd had been shouting and yelling. Now it was dead silent. The man with the key stepped toward an iron barred, low, red door and unlocked the great sliding bar. He lifted it and stepped back. The door swung open. The man hid behind it. Inside it was dark.

Then, ducking his head as he came up out of the dark pen, a bull came into the arena. He came out all in a rush, big, black and white, weighing over a ton and moving with a soft gallop. Just as he came out the sun seemed to dazzle him for an instant. He stood as though he were frozen, his great crest of muscle up, firmly planted, his eyes looking around, his horns pointed forward, black and white and sharp as porcupine quills. Then he charged. And as he charged I suddenly saw what bull fighting is all about.

For the bull was absolutely unbelievable. He seemed like some great prehistoric animal, absolutely deadly and absolutely vicious. And he was silent. He charged silently and with a soft galloping rush. When he turned he turned on his four feet like a cat. When he charged the first thing that caught his eye was a picador on one of the wretched horses. The picador dug his spurs into the horse and they galloped away.

The bull came on in his rush, refused to be shaken off, and in full gallop crashed into the animal from the side, ignored the horse, drove one of his horns high into the thigh of the picador, and tore him, saddle and all, off the horse's back.

The bull went on without pausing to worry the picador lying on the ground. The next picador was sitting his horse braced to receive the shock of the charge, his lance ready. The bull hit him sideways on, and horse and rider went high up in the air in a kicking mass and fell across the bull's back. As they came down the bull charged into them. The dough-faced kid, Chicuelo, vaulted over the fence, ran toward the bull and flopped his cape into the bull's face. The bull charged the cape and Chicuelo dodged backwards and had the bull clear in the arena.

Without an instant's hesitation the bull charged Chicuelo. The kid stood his ground, simply swung back on his heels and floated his cape like a ballet dancer's skirt into the bull's face as he passed.

"Ole!" — pronounced Oh-Lay! — roared the crowd.

THE bull whirled and charged again. Without moving Chicuelo repeated the performance. His legs rigid, just withdrawing his body from the rush of the bull's horns and floating the cape out with that beautiful swing.

Again the crowd roared. The Kid did this seven times. Each time the bull missed him by inches. Each time he gave the bull a free shot at him. Each time the crowd roared. Then he flopped the cape once at the bull at the finish of a pass, swung it around behind him and walked away from the bull to the barrera.

"He's the boy with the cape all right," said the Gin Bottle King. "That swing he did with the cape's called a Veronica."

The chubby faced Kid who did not like bull fighting and had just done the seven wonderful Veronicas was standing against the fence just below us. His face glistened with sweat in the sun but was almost expressionless. His eyes were looking out across the arena where the bull was standing making up his mind to charge a picador. He was studying the bull because a few minutes later it would be his duty to kill him, and once he went out with his thin, red-hilted sword and his piece of red cloth to kill the bull in the final act it would be him or the bull. There are no drawn battles in bull fighting.

I am not going to describe the rest of that afternoon in detail. It was the first bull fight I ever saw, but it was not the best. The best was in the little town of Pamplona, high up in the hills of Navarre, and came weeks later. Up in Pamplona, where they have held six days of bull fighting each year since 1126 A.D., and where the bulls race through the streets of the town each morning at six o'clock with half of the town running ahead of them. Pamplona, where every man and boy in town is an amateur bull fighter and where there is an amateur fight each morning that is attended by 20,000 people in which the amateur fighters are all unarmed and there is a casualty list at least equal to a Dublin election. But Pamplona, with the best bull fight and the wild tale of the amateur fights, comes in the second chapter.

I am not going to apologize for bull fighting. It is a survival of the days of the Roman Coliseum. But it does need some explanation. Bull fighting is not a sport. It was never supposed to be. It is a tragedy. A very great tragedy. The tragedy is the death of the bull. It is played in three definite acts.

The Gin Bottle King—who, by the way, does not drink gin—told us a lot of this that first night as we sat in the upstairs room of the little restaurant that made a specialty of roast young suckling pig, roasted on an oak plank and served with a mushroom tortilla and vino rioja. The rest we learned later on at the bull fighters' pensione in the Via San Jeronimo, where one of the bull fighters had eyes exactly like a rattlesnake.

Much of it we learned in the sixteen fights we saw in different parts of Spain from San Sebastien to Granada.

At any rate bull fighting is not a sport. It is a tragedy, and it symbolizes the struggle between man and the beasts. There are usually six bulls to a fight. A fight is called a corrida de tores. Fighting bulls are bred like race horses, some of the oldest breeding establishments being several hundred years old. A good bull is worth about $2,000. They are bred for speed, strength and viciousness. In other words a good fighting bull is an absolutely incorrigible bad bull.

BULL fighting is an exceedingly dangerous occupation. In sixteen fights I saw there were only two in which there was no one badly hurt. On the other hand it is very remunerative. A popular espada gets $5,000 for his afternoon's work. An unpopular espada though may not get $500. Both run the same risks. It is a good deal like Grand Opera for the really great matadors except that they run the chance of being killed every time they cannot hit high C.

No one at any time in the fight can approach the bull at any time except directly from the front. That is where the danger comes. There are also all sorts of complicated passes that must be done with the cape, each requiring as much technique as a champion billiard player. And underneath it all is the necessity for playing the old tragedy in the absolutely custom bound, law-laid-down way. It must all be done gracefully, seemingly effortlessly and always with dignity. The worst criticism the Spaniards ever make of a bull fighter is that his work is "vulgar."

The three absolute acts of the tragedy are first the entry of the bull when the picadores receive the shock of his attacks and attempt to protect their horses with their lances. Then the horses go out and the second act is the planting of the banderillos. This is one of the most interesting and difficult parts but among the easiest for a new bull fight fan to appreciate in technique. The banderillos are three foot, gaily colored darts with a small fish hook prong in the end. The man who is going to plant them walks out into the arena alone with the bull. He lifts the banderillos at arm's length and points them toward the bull. Then he calls "Toro! Toro!" The bull charges and the banderillero rises to his toes, bends in a curve forward and just as the bull is about to hit him drops the darts into the bull's hump just back of his horns.

They must go in evenly, one on each side. They must not be shoved, or thrown or stuck in from the side. This is the first time the bull has been completely baffled, there is the prick of the darts that he cannot escape and there are no horses for him to charge into. But he charges the man again and again and each time he gets a pair of the long banderillos that hang from his hump by their tiny barbs and flop like porcupine quills.

Last is the death of the bull, which is in the hands of the matador who has had charge of the bull since his first attack. Each matador has two bulls in the afternoon. The death of the bull is most formal and can only be brought about in one way, directly from the front by the matador who must receive the bull in full charge and kill him with a sword thrust between the shoulders just back of the neck and between the horns. Before killing the bull he must first do a series of passes with the muleta, a piece of red cloth he carries about the size of a large napkin. With the muleta the torero must show his complete mastery of the bull, must make the bull miss him again and again by inches, before he is allowed to kill him. It is in this phase that most of the fatal accidents occur.

The word "Toreador" is obsolete Spanish and is never used. The torero is usually called an Espada or swordsman. He must be proficient in all three acts of the fight. In the first he uses the cape and does veronicas and protects the picadors by taking the bull out and away from them when they are spilled to the ground. In the second act he plants the banderillos. In the third act he masters the bull with the muleta and kills him.

Few toreros excel in all three departments. Some, like young Chicuelo, are unapproachable in their cape work. Others like the late Joselito are wonderful banderilleros. Only a few are great killers. Most of the greatest killers are gypsies.

(To be Concluded.)

A Royal Rage In A Fitting Room

A True Tale of An Unconventional Happening in a Large Toronto Store.

By GERTRUDE E. S. PRINGLE

SCENE, fitting-room in imported dress section of large Toronto store, where a lady, having removed her outer garments, is standing in mauve silk bloomers and torchon lace brassiere, with a saleswoman about to try on a French frock. Door opens, and in enter two massive women and a second saleswoman carrying armful of beaded dresses.

Lady, haughtily: "Excuse me. This room is occupied."

Newly entered saleswoman: "Pardon, but we have to use it, too, as there isn't a vacant one."

Lady: "I protest. You must all go out at once. I will not be crowded in this way when I come to choose a dress."

First intruder: "I guess we're as good as you are."

Second intruder: "Who do you think you are anyway—Queen Mary?"

They both calmly disrobe, while their saleswoman prepares to try on the dresses.

Lady, with angry dignity: "Very well. If you won't leave, I will, and I'll see the manager about this." Exit hurriedly.

First saleswoman, rushing after her: "Pardon, but Madame has forgotten her clothes."

Lady (oblivious of everything but her grievance, and quite unconscious of her unique appearance in bloomers and brassiere), addressing a young man: "Are you the manager?"

"No, Madame. I'm the assistant manager."

Lady: "Very well. I demand that you put those odious fat creatures out of my fitting-room. I was about to select a dress and they crowded in. I refuse to try on before them. Order them out at once, please."

Assistant manager: "I'm very sorry, Madame, but it is necessary to have two fittings in the one room when we are so busy as to-day."

Lady, furiously: "Very well. I want to see the manager at once. Send him to me, and the general manager and the board of directors. Do you hear?"

"Order them out at once, please."

Assistant manager, entirely subdued: "Certainly, Madame."

He goes, and soon returns with a decisive looking, keen-eyed man.

Lady: "Are you the manager or general manager of this place?"

Man: "I'm the manager of this department, Madame. What can I do for you?"

Lady: "I demand that you clear my fitting-room of those two fat women who pushed in when I got it first. I will not stand such treatment. If I cannot have a room to myself when I am getting a hundred-dollar frock I'll go to the store opposite in future. They know how to treat their customers there. These women are greasy-looking and reek of cheap perfume, and it is an outrage to be treated this way, and I won't stand it, and if they are not instantly turned out this is the last time I ever enter your shop, and my business is worth having, and I never was so annoyed in my life, and I"—pauses for breath.

Manager, soothingly: "Indeed, there has been a mistake made. They had no business to enter your fitting-room when you were using it. The saleswoman should have known better and made them wait. Just show me the room, and I'll see you have it to yourself."

Lady prances ahead to her fitting-room. Manager knocks and sternly orders everyone to vacate at once and wait for an empty room.

Exit, casting angry looks behind, two fat brunets in beaded dresses, and a depressed saleswoman. Lady, still unconscious of her bloomers and brassiere, triumphantly takes possession, and renews her trying-on of frocks.

Hip, Hip, Hippocampus!

WHEREAS most fishes pay little attention to their offspring, merely depositing their spawn in suitable spawning beds and leaving the young fry to care for itself when the eggs hatch, the seahorse is a most devoted and painstaking parent.

This fish is provided, in fact, with a pouch similar to that of the kangaroo. In this pouch the eggs are deposited and remain until hatched and some little time afterward.

However, it is not the mother fish who possesses this convenient receptable, but the father! Once her eggs have been laid the duties of Madame Hippocampus are at an end.

It is her spouse who carries the eggs about with him during their period of incubation and until the babes are strong enough to escape from his capacious pocket, which is situated on the abdomen, at the root of his long, curving tail.—Detroit News.

After 1919, Montmartre became the meeting place for American expatriates

to his various friends in Paris. Among them was one which was to play an important part in Hemingway's further development. It was addressed to Gertrude Stein, an American novelist whose role as discoverer and patroness of struggling artists and poets from Picasso to James Joyce far outshone her literary significance. During the 'twenties her 'salon' was a symbol of literary Paris.

The author Ford Madox Ford described the youth of America stampeding from the western prairies like high-spirited colts when the barrier between arid and green pastures is lifted. They filled the Paris Boulevards, and their continual restlessness was dizzying.

'A lost generation.' Gertrude Stein coined the phrase. She meant a youth which, uprooted during the storm of war, now allowed itself to be blown like chaff through the early years of peace; drowned its disillusion in alcohol; slept away the days and shared its bed with a different partner each night. Gigolos

'A rose is a rose is a rose.'
Gertrude Stein's style influenced Hemingway

and nymphomaniacs, homosexuals and Lesbians rubbed shoulders. Montparnasse was their stamping ground, with the Café Rotonde as their favourite meeting place.

Hemingway became their chronicler, although, contrary to the impression gained from his works by many critics and readers, he never belonged to that generation. Moreover, he never intended to be their spokesman. 'Magnificent bombast', he called Gertrude Stein's phrase. He did not agree with her, as he did not feel lost. In 1957 he wrote to his biographer, Carlos Baker: 'I thought the generation beat-up, maybe, . . . in many ways. But damned if we were lost except for deads, *gueules cassées,* and certified crazies. Lost, no. And Criqui, who was a real *gueule cassée,* won the featherweight championship of the world. We were a very solid generation, though without education (some of us.) But you could always get it.'

In an article for the 'Star' he reported on his first visit to the Café Rotonde thus: 'This is a strange-acting and strange-looking breed that crowd the tables of the Café Rotonde. They are nearly all loafers expending the energy that an

The Café de la Paix,
a Mecca for
American tourists

Ezra Pound, friend and
adviser to the
young Hemingway

artist puts into his creative work in talking about what they are going to do and condemning the work of all artists who have gained any degree of recognition. By talking about art they obtain the same satisfaction that the real artist does in his work.'

Hemingway soon discovered that, as well as dilettantes, misunderstood geniuses and work-shy Bohemians, Montparnasse — even the Café Rotonde — also had true artists. Two of these became his closest friends and advisors: Gertrude Stein and Ezra Pound.

Gertrude Stein was always the first to read his stories and poems. He would visit her every few days and listen attentively as she expounded her theories on style and language. She said that she found the young man 'extraordinarily good-looking and in every way more European than American'. She praised various stories of his, advising him nevertheless to start from the beginning and concentrate exclusively on his work. She thought it would be better for him to give up his journalistic activity. Hemingway realised the truth of this, but could not afford to do anything about it for the time being.

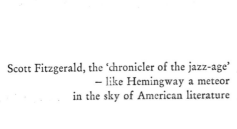

James Joyce, the high priest
of the moderns

Scott Fitzgerald, the 'chronicler of the jazz-age'
– like Hemingway a meteor
in the sky of American literature

Ezra Pound was the first to recognise Hemingway's great talents. This pioneer of modern American poetry became his best friend. Ernest was loyal to him until Pound's political views, his anti-semitic and fascist leanings, destroyed the friendship. Apart from Pound's literary judgement and his practical advice, Hemingway esteemed the tireless way in which he was always prepared to help aspiring young authors.

'Only a fifth of his energy he devoted to his own work,' Hemingway wrote in an appreciation of Pound. 'With the rest of his time he tries to advance the fortunes, both material and artistic, of his friends. He defends them when they are attacked, he gets them into magazines and out of jail. He loans them money. He sells their pictures. He arranges concerts for them. He writes articles about them. He introduces them to wealthy women. He gets publishers to take their books. He sits up all night with them when they claim to be dying and he witnesses their wills. He advances them hospital expenses and dissuades them from suicide. And in the end a few of them refrain from knifing him at the first opportunity.'

Gertrude Stein and Ezra Pound were his tutors. Pound read each one of his stories and returned them with remarks and detailed suggestions. Gertrude Stein confined herself to a more general criticism, always constructive and sometimes harsh. In his memoirs of those years Hemingway says that 'Ezra was right half the time, and when he was wrong he was so wrong you were never in any doubt about it. Gertrude was always right.'

Hemingway's journalistic commitments demanded much travelling. Europe was in a state of great political and social upheaval. In September 1922 Mussolini marched on Rome, in October Kemal Pasha drove the Greeks out of

1922: Mussolini marches on Rome – Hemingway smells danger for Europe

The murder of Socialist
Matteotti swings Hemingway towards
anti-fascism

Asia, in January 1923 the French occupied the Ruhr. At the Genoa Conference
in 1922, Hemingway had gained an insight into the bustle and intrigue of high
politics. He was one of the first to warn against the fatal danger of Fascism.
At a time when many American correspondents — and even European statesmen — considered Mussolini a great man, who did nothing worse than bring
order and education to the lazy and undisciplined Italians and who saw that
the trains ran on time, Hemingway wrote him off as an out-and-out scoundrel,
the biggest bluffer in Europe. He considered it childish and stupid to compare
Mussolini with Napoleon. He likened him instead to Horatio Bottomley, the
English financier and M.P. who had just received a seven-year prison sentence
for fraudulent conversion of public funds. He described the Duce as an effective
orator, an unscrupulous demagogue who covered his shady deals with the cloak
of patriotism. On the other hand, Hemingway also warned against under-esti-
mating Mussolini. 'Bottomley was a fool. Mussolini isn't a fool and he is a
great organizer.'

The murder of Matteotti, the Socialist leader who paid for his dis-
closures of the corruption and barbarity of Fascism with his life, confirmed
Hemingway as an anti-fascist. He remained one for the rest of his life, yet
without subscribing to Communism. Political ideologies did not interest him.

What did worry him constantly was 'man's inhumanity to man', the raging of man against himself. He could never get away from this subject.

He had ample opportunity to study man's cruelty when he joined the Greek civilians on their flight to Macedonia in October 1922. Scenes that could have been taken from Dante left him with even more horrifying impressions than those he gained at the Italian front. Goya's *The Disasters of War* provided a clear example for his Greek reports, which were, in fact, the high-light of his journalistic career, for even in his later war reports he never surpassed their realism, significance and perspicuity. His articles already disclosed the form and style of future short stories. One only has to read his descriptions of a street fight in Cologne, which appeared in the 'Star Weekly' in September 1922:

'A Cologne mob attempted to dislodge a huge equestrian statue of William Hohenzollern — in a brawl that started to be a revolution and ended in a small-sized riot.' During the attack on the statue, Hemingway explained, a police officer appeared. 'The mob threw the policeman into the river. In the cold, swift swirl of the Rhine against the base of the bridge the policeman hung on to one of the abutments and shouted up that he knew who was in the mob and

Conference of Genoa (1922): Hemingway wins his spurs as a reporter

Summit conference, 1922 model: Tête-à-tête between Lloyd George (second from the left) and Barthou

would see that they were all punished. So the mob swarmed down and tried to push the policeman loose into the current. It meant drowning for the policeman to let go — and he hung on. Then the mob chopped his fingers loose from the stone with the hatchet with which they had been attacking the statue.'

Five years later Hemingway described an equally brutal scene in his famous short story *An Idyll in the Alps*. In his news stories Hemingway was already using the highly individual style — indirect speech, jerky telegraphese — which he later used with such great effect in his novel *The Sun Also Rises*.

During the occupation of the Ruhr he described his meeting with four French soldiers in Kehl:

Hemingway's experiences in Germany: Separationist disturbances during the Ruhr occupation

French troops on the Ruhr – grist to Hitler's mill

'One of them told me there would be a train at 11.15 for Offenburg, a military tram; it was about half an hour to Offenburg, but this droll train would get there about two o'clock. He grinned. Monsieur was from Paris? What did Monsieur think about the match Criqui — Zjawnny Kilbane? Ah. He had thought very much the same. He had always had the idea he was no fool, this Kilbane. The military service? Well, it was all the same. It made no difference where one did it. In two months now he would be through. It was a shame he was not free, perhaps we could have a talk together. Monsieur had seen this Kilbane box? The new wine was not bad at the buffet. But after all he was on guard. The buffet is straight down the corridor, if Monsieur leaves the baggage here it will be all right.'

Hemingway constructed the report as if it were a short story, the bar scene providing the climax. He avoided the naturalistic rendering of dialogue and all personal comment:

'In the buffet was a sad-looking waiter in a dirty shirt... a long bar and two forty-year-old French second lieutenants sitting at a table in the corner. I bowed as I entered, and they both saluted.

' "No," the waiter said, "there is no milk. You can have black coffee, but it is ersatz coffee. The beer is good."

'The waiter sat down at the table. "No, there is no one here now," he said. "All the people you say you saw in July cannot come now. The French will not give them passports to come into Germany."

The Ruhr 1923: a Witches' Sabbath for the Nationalists

'"How do they get along with the French here in town?"
'"No trouble. They are good people. Just like us. Some of them are nasty
sometimes, but they are good people. Nobody hates, except profiteers. They had
something to lose. We haven't had any fun since 1914. If you make any money
it gets no good, and there is only to spend it. That is what we do. Some day it
will be over. I don't know how. Last year I had enough money saved up to
buy a *gasthaus* in Hernberg; now that money wouldn't buy four bottles of
champagne."

'There was a shrill peep of a whistle outside. I paid and shook hands with the
waiter, saluted the two forty-year-old second lieutenants, who were now playing checkers at their table, went out to take the military train to Offenburg.'

The changes Hemingway made when transcribing his articles into short
stories are interesting. Here is a report as it appeared in the 'Toronto Star' in
October 1922:

Tanks against the coal mines: Hemingway studied the psychology of both the occupiers and the occupied

'In a never-ending, staggering march the Christian population of Eastern Thrace is jamming the roads towards Macedonia. The main column crossing the Maritza River at Adrianople is twenty miles long. Twenty miles of carts drawn by cows, bullocks and muddy-flanked water buffalo, with exhausted, staggering men, women and children, blankets over their heads, walking blindly in the rain beside their worldly goods.

'The main stream is being swelled from all the back country. They don't know where they are going. They left their farms, villages and ripe, brown fields and joined the main stream of refugees when they heard the Turk was coming. Now they can only keep their places in the ghastly procession while mud-plashed Greek cavalry herd them along like cow-punchers driving steers.

'It is a silent procession. Nobody even grunts. It is all they can do to keep moving. The brilliant peasant costumes are soaked and draggled. Chickens dangle by their feet from the carts. Calves muzzle at the draught cattle wher-

Hemingway's next mission: the war in
Asia. His reports from the Graeco-Turkish front
became literary narratives

ever a jam halts the stream. An old man marches bent under a young pig, a scythe and a gun, with a chicken tied to his scythe. A husband spreads a blanket over a woman in labour in one of the carts to keep off the driving rain. She is the only person making a sound. Her little daughter looks at her in horror and begins to cry. And the procession keeps moving.'

In the adaptation a year later Hemingway described the same scene thus:

'Minarets stuck up in the rain out of Adrianople across the mud flats. The carts were jammed for thirty miles along the Karagatch road. Water buffalo and cattle were hauling carts through the mud. No end and no beginning. Just carts loaded with everything they owned. The old men and women, soaked through, walked along keeping the cattle moving. The Maritza was running yellow almost up to the bridge. Carts were jammed solid on the bridge with camels bobbing along through them. Greek cavalry herded along the procession. Women and kids were in the carts crouched with mattresses, mirrors, sewing machines, bundles. There was a woman having a kid with a young girl holding a blanket over her and crying. Scared sick looking at it. It rained all through the evacuation.'

In his book *The Apprenticeship of Ernest Hemingway* Charles A. Fenton compares the two interpretations and points out that in the story adaptation Hemingway has left out most of the adjectives. This was in sharp contrast to the first description, which although clear and precise contained almost thirty adjectives. In this first description Hemingway played on the reader's emotions. 'They do not know where they are going', he wrote of the refugees. He consciously tried to arouse the reader's sympathy for the fugitives. He had the same object when describing the colourful peasant costumes which now clung wetly to their bodies. In the final adaptation he omitted all description and made the

Ivan Turgenev, the young
Hemingway's favourite
Russian author

report more objective. Thus he erased the figure of the husband, only the young
girl remained, thereby accentuating the horror of the situation. Now there is
not even a father who could comfort the child.

Hemingway's articles in the 'Toronto Star' caused a sensation. He had succeeded as a journalist and reporter, but this did not satisfy him. He wanted to be
an author, to write stories and novels. In this field, though, he was unlucky.
Publishers refused his short stories on the ground that they were 'not stories'.
They were indeed sketches, more an American version of Turgenev's *Poems in
Prose*. He admired Turgenev and Tolstoy more than any other classical Russian
authors. 'I love *War and Peace*' he once said, 'for the wonderful, penetrating,
and true descriptions of war and of people but I have never believed in the
great Count's thinking. I wish there could have been someone in his confidence
with authority to remove his heaviest and worst thinking and keep him simply
inventing truly. He could invent with more insight and truth than anyone who
ever lived. But his ponderous and Messianic thinking was no better than that of
any other evangelical professor of history, and I learned from him to distrust
my Thinking with a capital T and try to write as truly, as straightly, as objectively and as humbly as possible.'

The bull was stronger: Hemingway tried his hand at being a matador in Pamplona in 1924. His first wife, Hadley Richardson, was watching him

TORONTO WRITER GORED BY ANGRY BULL IN SPAIN

Ernest Hemingway, formerly foreign correspondent of The Toronto Star and member of the local staff, was recently gored by an angry bull, during the annual fiesta at Pamplona, Spain. He received only painful bruises from the bull's bandaged horns, while his companion, Donald Ogden Stewart, an American newspaper correspondent, suffered two broken ribs. Above is shown Mr. Hemingway, with his wife, who is in Europe with him.

BULL GORES TORONTO WRITER IN ANNUAL PAMPLONA FIESTA

But Only Badly Bruised — Companion, However, Had Two Ribs Broken—Ernest Hemingway Recently on the Staff of The Star

Special to The Star by United Press

Paris, July 30.—Two young American writers from the colony here were gored by a bull at Pamplona, Spain, during the course of the annual fiesta.

A party of four, consisting of Donald Ogden Stewart, Ernest Hemingway, Robert McAlmon and John Dos Passos (author of "Soldiers Three"), left here some time ago for a Spanish tour having Pamplona as its chief objective. At that place it is the custom every year to drive a herd of bulls through the barricaded street to the arena. The animals are pursued by the youth of the town, who later bait and fight them in the bull ring, without using any weapons. Escape from injury depends upon the youths' agility.

Both Stewart and Hemingway participated in the first day of the sports without meeting mishap. On the second, however, Stewart was thrown by a bull, but, undaunted, wagered Hemingway he could return, ride the wild beast, blow smoke in its eyes and finally wrestle and throw it.

When he was preparing to launch upon this enterprise, a toreador presented him with a red cape. Before he had finished shaking hands with his Spanish backer, a bull had charged him, hoisted him on its horns, rolled him over and finally hurled him into the air. When he crashed down, the enraged animal tried to gore him.

Hemingway ran to the rescue and was also gored but, owing to the fact that the bulls used in this annual carnival have their horns bandaged, he suffered only painful bruises. Stewart had two ribs broken.

Ernest Hemingway is familiar to readers of The Toronto Star through European cables and correspondence which he has contributed to this paper. He covered the Genoa and Lausanne conferences for The Star and interviewed many of the most prominent statesmen of Europe. Last autumn and winter he was here in this city working on the staff of The Toronto Daily Star and later The Star Weekly.

Mr. Hemingway, who is a son of Dr. C. E. Hemingway, 600 North Kenilworth avenue, Oak Park, Chicago, served during the war as a lieutenant with the A. E. F. in Italy. He was the first American wounded on that front and was awarded two war crosses and a silver medal.

Leo Tolstoy. Hemingway
greatly admired him

When compiling a list of books which he considered priceless he included
two of Tolstoy's novels — *Anna Karenina* and *War and Peace*, — Dostoievsky's
The Brothers Karamazov, and 'all of Turgenev's works'.

The other works on the list were Mark Twain's *Huckleberry Finn*, the short
stories of Henry James and Sherwood Anderson, *Ulysses* and *The Dubliners*
by James Joyce and the autobiography of Yeats. English books he named were
Wuthering Heights and Hudson's *Far Way and Long Ago*, two novels by Henry
Fielding, three by Captain Marryat and Kipling's short stories. From French

Hemingway's second book,
In Our Time. 170 copies
were sold

literature he chose Stendhal's *The Scarlet and the Black*, *Madame Bovary* by Flaubert and Maupassant's *The House of Madame Tellier;* and from German literature the novel *Buddenbrooks* by Thomas Mann.

Hemingway's desire to combine journalism with fruitful literary activity was not fulfilled. He found he had neither the time nor the concentration for his serious work. In addition there were the everlasting financial worries. His earnings from his newspaper reports barely kept body and soul together.

In January 1923, the 'Star' sent him to Lausanne to report on the international

Personalities from Hemingway's
reports: Kemal Atatürk
as diplomat –

conference which was to settle the Graeco-Turkish conflict. After a week he
wanted to return to Paris as life in Switzerland was too expensive. His expenses
were not to be paid until later and his fee did not even cover his hotel bill. An
American colleague secured him a lucrative side-line: Hemingway became correspondent of the Hearst news agency.

For three reasons this stay in Lausanne was an important one for Hemingway.
While there, he became friendly with the correspondent of 'The Manchester
Guardian', William Bolitho. Bolitho was a brilliant reporter with a sound and
comprehensive grasp of politics – and it was in this sphere in particular that
Hemingway lacked the basic knowledge for a true understanding of European
events. His historical, sociological and economic knowledge was distinctly
slight. Bolitho helped him to fill in the gaps.

– and as people's tribune

The second incident which made the visit to Lausanne so important for Hemingway was less fortunate. A suitcase which contained the manuscripts of all the stories he had written during the previous years, in addition to a half-finished novel of which he held high hopes, was stolen from his wife at the Gare de Lyon on the way from Paris to Lausanne. Hemingway did not possess any copies of his work and the manuscripts were never found. It was a heavy blow, one to which he never became entirely reconciled.

In contrast, the third incident connected with the Lausanne mission was the lucky break Hemingway had so ardently prayed for. On the return journey to Paris the young couple visited Ezra Pound who had settled in Rapallo. Also visiting him was Robert McAlmon, a young American who owned a small publishing house in Paris which put out books by *avant garde* authors.

Pound persuaded McAlmon to publish a collection of Hemingway's short stories. Under the title *Three Stories and Ten Poems* the book contained two stories which Hemingway had offered to periodicals, thereby eluding the thief in Paris, and also one which he had just finished. During previous months seven of the poems had been printed in *Poetry*, a small literary review.

This small volume appeared in August 1923, shortly before Hemingway's twenty-fourth birthday. The edition consisted of 300 copies. Financial success was non-existent. However, it was Hemingway's first book and aroused admiration in literary circles. Edmund Wilson, one of the most respected of American critics, discussed it several months later together with a second volume of Hemingway's sketches, which had been issued in 1924 by another *avant garde* publisher, William Bird. This 32-page volume was entitled *In Our Time* and

Sylvia Beach, the proprietress
of the bookshop 'Shakespeare
and Co.' in Paris

Archibald MacLeish arrived in Paris
in 1923 — 'my life began here',
he declared. He greatly helped and
encouraged Hemingway in his literary career

contained the best sketches and episodes from his journalistic expeditions. The edition was even smaller than that of his first work — only 170 copies were printed.

All material difficulties and disappointments were compensated for by the artistic inspiration he gained in Paris from meetings with poets and artists who like himself had left America, and formed a colony of expatriates. Among these John Dos Passos, Malcolm Cowley, Archibald MacLeish and Scott Fitzgerald were his particular friends — all men on the road to fame; a few years later they were all recognised as the representatives of modern American literature. Meetings took place in the cafés of Montparnasse, in Ezra Pound's studio or in the book-shop 'Shakespeare and Co.' which a young American girl, Sylvia Beach — also an expatriate — had opened in the vicinity of the Odeon Theatre immedi-

The birthplace of the novel
Ulysses: its creator, James
Joyce (left), and its first publisher,
Sylvia Beach (centre), in the
'Shakespeare and Co.' book-shop

Hemingway's first publisher,
Robert McAlmon: literature was for him
an unsuccessful venture

ately after the war. Her first author was James Joyce. She published his *Ulysses*
after its appearance in the magazine *Little Revue,* when it was banned in
America, England and Ireland as immoral and obscene.

In spite of his intensive work, Hemingway remained faithful to his old love
of sport. He was a regular spectator at boxing matches and six-days bycicle
races, and trained several times a week with professional boxers.

This mode of life was abruptly interrupted in the summer of 1923. Hadley
became pregnant. As Alice B. Toklas, Gertrude Stein's secretary and confidante,
writes in her autobiography: 'Hemingway turned up alone. He came to the
house about ten o'clock in the morning and he stayed, he stayed for lunch, he
stayed all afternoon, he stayed for dinner and he stayed until about ten o'clock
at night and then all of a sudden he announced that his wife was *enceinte* and
then with great bitterness, and I, I am too young to be a father. We consoled
him as best we could and sent him on his way.'

Literary 'salons'
in the Paris
of the 'twenties:

Ezra Pound's studio
(from left to right:
Pound, John Quinn, Ford
Madox Ford, James Joyce)

Gertrude Stein's studio
(Alice B. Toklas
left, and
Gertrude Stein)

Wounded again:
Hemingway and his publisher,
Sylvia Beach, in front of
'Shakespeare and Co.'

A few days later Ernest and Hadley came to see Gertrude Stein. Ernest explained that he had decided to return to America. There he would work hard for a year and earn enough money from his newspaper articles to give up journalism. Then he would settle in Paris and live as a free writer.

As promised, the Hemingways were back in Paris five months later. There were now three: Ernest, Hadley and the twelve-week-old John.

On the brink
of success:
Hemingway
in Paris, 1924

The next two years marked the turning-point in Hemingway's life and work.
Several of his short stories were accepted by French magazines, the *Querschnitt*
of Berlin printed a number of his sketches and also a longer story, *The Bullfight*.
Shortly afterwards he at long last found favour in America. 'Atlantic Monthly',
the leading literary journal, accepted his story *Fifty Grand*. From then onwards
American magazines sought his contributions, and the editor of a Hearst paper

Madame Shakespeare
To M. Shakespeare et Co
12 rue de l'Odeon

The Paris Post Office
located Madame Shakespeare: Hemingway
was writing to Sylvia Beach

offered him a contract which would have guaranteed his financial security for
years. Hemingway declined. He feared, as he said, that his work would suffer
if he knew that everything he wrote was already accepted and paid for. 'The
integrity in a writer is like virginity in a woman,' he said, 'once lost, it is never
recovered.' So he struggled on, but kept his integrity.

In the meantime his marriage had broken up. Hadley left him. He lived
in straitened circumstances in a small room sparsely furnished with a bed and
a table, he ate only one meal a day and that mostly a plate of roast potatoes.
Hunger was his constant companion.

Two of this friends, Sherwood Anderson and Scott Fitzgerald, came to
Hemingway's assistance. Scott Fitzgerald, the prodigy of American literature,
the adored chronicler of the Jazz Age, had read Hemingway's latest works. He
extolled them to his publisher, Scribner, and his influential lector, Maxwell
Perkins. At the same time Anderson persuaded the publishers Bone and Liveright to offer Hemingway a contract. Ernest was to receive an advance of two
hundred dollars in return for a selection of short stories, but he also had to
guarantee the publishers first refusal on his next three books. Hemingway immediately accepted this offer.

The stories again appeared under the title *In Our Time*. The volume contained
all the sketches in the Paris edition with ten new stories added. They were
interspersed with short *Miniatures* which illustrated in contrapuntal fashion the
chronological background of the stories. A similar technique was used by Dos
Passos in his trilogy *Manhattan Transfer*, in which he continually interrupted
the plot with newspaper articles and items of news. Hemingway's book was

The
successful
author

After his first successes Hemingway begins to
indulge his enthusiasms. He firmly
demonstrates his male ideals,
until Hemingway the man becomes a legend

favourably received by the critics but was not a popular success. The publishers
had difficulty in getting rid of the first edition of 1,300 copies.

Hemingway was disappointed but not discouraged. He had just finished the
rough draft of his first novel. Before he started rewriting it — a work which
for him always meant deep and nerve-racking concentration — he wished to
free his mind of it for a while and to 'relax'; so during the next eight days he
wrote *Torrents of Spring*, a satire on the contemporary literary scene. He sent
the manuscript to Liveright who returned it a few days later.

Hemingway must have expected this refusal. In *Torrents of Spring* he had
ridiculed not only Mencken and Gertrude Stein, but also Sherwood Anderson's
style and 'solidness'. Anderson was Liveright's star author.

Scribner, on the other hand, accepted the manuscript and published it in May
1926, although admittedly without illusions about the possibility of a success.
By doing this, however, he hoped to secure the rights of Hemingway's next
novel, from which Maxwell Perkins expected much.

It was a good speculation. *Torrents of Spring* did not even create a *success
de scandale* and only resulted in Hemingway losing the friendship of Anderson
and Gertrude Stein. However the great, now rewritten novel, *The Sun Also
Rises*, gained Hemingway fame overnight, laid the foundation of his literary
career and opened a new chapter in American literature.

Archibald MacLeish later described Hemingway's meteoric rise to fame in
one of his poems: 'A veteran of the war before he was twenty; famous at
twenty-five; at thirty a master.'

The tremendous success of *The Sun Also Rises* can be explained in various
ways. First there is the plot itself — unusually 'shocking'. Sex has an unfailing
magnetism for the reading public and the novel is full of it. Lady Ashley
Bratt is portrayed as beautiful, intelligent, unconventional and discontented,

Film fame follows
literary fame in
A Farewell to Arms
(Gary Cooper and Helen
Hayes in the closing scene)

passing from lover to lover. The one man who could save her from herself, Jake Barnes, is sexually impotent. He endures his fate with dignity and strength; she vainly seeks oblivion in alcohol and in the arms of her other suitors. Her fiancé, Mike Campbell, is as unprincipled and malcontent as she. Robert Cohn is a neurotic, whose love for her is like an incurable illness. Only the bullfighter, Pedro Romero, is 'all man' and conforms to Ashley's idea of the ideal lover — unbeaten in the arena, indomitable in bed. However, she renounces him rather than destroy him or sully his youthful purity. The colourful background against which the story develops heightens its effect. The cafés of Montparnasse, a Spanish town during a fiesta — colourful, exotic and sultry, an intoxicating

Tyrone Power in the film *The Sun also Rises*

atmosphere. Over everything hangs a cloud of alcoholic vapour and the stench of death.

Yet the novel's especial effect is not drawn from these external elements, but from its theme, which forms the basis of the events and determines the actions of the characters. Lady Bratt and Jake Barnes are both victims of war, victims of the age. The war had killed Ashley's first great love and deprived Jake of virility. War had made them what they were. Campbell and Cohn are representatives of a generation lost and cracking under the confusion of the age. This was not typical of the whole generation, certainly not; but this hopelessness, this feeling of being lost, this tired cynicism were shared by millions of

Odd-man-out of society: Humphrey Bogart in the film *To Have and Have Not*

young people. To this extent Lady Bratt and her friends are typical of the period, and their fate is of almost symbolic validity. *The Sun Also Rises* became the Bible of the 'lost generation'. Lady Bratt and her friends had models in the Bohemian circle in Paris; the initiated recognised the originals of Hemingway's characters among the wellknown clientèle of the Café Rotonde.

That the novel has not lost its power today, when the theme has less topicality and the comparison of the characters with their originals no longer holds any interest, testifies to its literary value and Hemingway's art. In language and in style, in the descriptions of nature and the characterization, Hemingway

Burt Lancaster in the ring *(The Killers)*

proved he was a master in his very first novel. Indeed, Lady Bratt is probably the best and most true-to-life female character he ever created.

A particular circumstance decided the novel's success in Germany. American literature was regarded, until the 'twenties, as of little account; in fact, it was barely known. Mark Twain, Walt Whitman, Edgar Allan Poe were 'classic', outsiders, great poets who happened to have been born in America. Names such as Henry James, Melville, Nathaniel Hawthorne, Stephen Crane, were known only to a small number of connoisseurs.

Significantly, it was Upton Sinclair who was responsible for the idea of Ame-

rican literature which was held in Germany; his sociological novels were regarded as typical of American writing. German tradition demanded that the poet remain above everyday life and that he should leave politics and economics to reporters. The poet had nobler missions in life — the exploration of the human soul, the study of the human heart. Naturalism had certainly broken with this tradition, yet the true poet was still expected to be a-political. Stock exchange, factory, slaughterhouse, the press were not worthy of his contemplation. Upton Sinclair opened up a range of subjects, hitherto *terra incognita* to the German reader, more strange than even the African jungle. This assured general interest and widespread popularity for his books. However, he did not count as as poet. 'America is not a poet's country.'

Then Hemingway appeared on the scene. He had the eye, the ear, the tracking

The Snows of Kilimanjaro:
hero in love and in danger
– Gregory Peck with Susan Hayward
(left) and Ava Gardner (right)

instinct of the reporter, but also the sensibility, the sympathetic psychological understanding, the language of the poet. Thus he furnished the formula for practically all American literature. Its individuality and originality were confirmed in that essayists and critics were able to find a formula at all. If European literature was 'old', American literature was 'young'. European literature was 'tired, plagued by doubts' — American literature was 'positive'. European writers were 'incorrigible Romantics' — Americans 'hard-boiled Realists'.

It was indeed wrong to reduce all American writing to a formula and thereby overlook the many different streams and directions to be found among these young authors. Also, the alleged antithesis between European and American literature was an arbitrary concept. The impression of America gained by European intellectuals was false. It was a myth, born of the self-hatred of the European thinker, and the 'love-hate' towards the technical age which America represented so completely. Not the European writers were tired, but the new generation was weary of Europe. It admired the 'factualism' of America because it had lost the belief in idealism and was ashamed of this loss. It covered its nakedness with the cloak of 'realism', but its realism was really nothing but a new form of romanticism.

Hemingway represented this romantic realism more completely than any other contemporary writer.

★

While Hemingway was working on his next novel, a new volume of his short stories, *Men Without Women,* was published. His new-found fame grew. However, it was not until his next novel that he achieved popular as well as critical acclaim, expressing itself in mass editions, film offers and an income which soon put him among the richest authors of our time.

The novel was called *A Farewell to Arms.* As the first novel reflected the confusion of the years after the war, Hemingway's second novel portrayed the paradox of war itself. As in the first novel there was no hope and no future for Lady Bratt and Jake, so Lieutenant Frederick Henry and Nurse Catherine Barkley became the victims of a cruel and hostile age. Their love story, which starts in a field hospital where the lieutenant is being treated for severe leg injuries, ends with Catherine's death. She dies in childbirth but it is actually the war which condemns them both to destruction. After the Italian defeat at Caporetto — one of the best and most thrilling battle scenes in world literature — the lieutenant becomes a deserter. He flees with his sweetheart to Switzerland, but they cannot escape despair and horror. Death is always at their backs and not to be cheated.

This novel is an unembellished chapter from Hemingway's own life. Not only does the lieutenant's fate correspond with his own — from the trenches, through injury, to the hospital — but Catherine's death was also inspired by personal experience.

A short time previously Hemingway had married for the second time, again a girl from St Louis, Pauline Pfeiffer, who was a fashion reporter on the Paris editorial staff of 'Vogue'. As Hemingway wrote in the foreword to a later edition of the novel, his second son, Patrick, was born while he was working on the first draft. It was a difficult birth and the mother had to have a Caesarian deliv-

The successful author's luxury villa: Key West in Florida

ery. Then, just as Hemingway was starting on the final draft, his father committed suicide.

'The fact that the book was a tragic one', Hemingway wrote, 'did not make me unhappy since I believed that life was a tragedy and knew it could only have one end.'

A Farewell to Arms was published in September 1929. Four months later 80,000 copies had been sold. The novel was dramatised and filmed. Hemingway settled in Key West, a small fishing port on the southern tip of Florida. He lived in high style, bought a yacht, indulged his passion for fishing and dedicated himself almost more to the *mise-en-scène* of his own life than to his art. Instead

Hemingway's wives: Pauline Pfeiffer

of creating heroes for his novels he himself became the hero of a legend during his lifetime.

For ten years his achievements in sport, his triumphs as hunter and fisherman, his eccentric sayings, the reports about his peculiar friends and his capacity for drink filled the columns of the American press. His literary output was less remarkable.

Like father, like sons: Hemingway hunting with Gregory (left) and Patrick (right). In the background: Mrs Gary Coope

Sons with no mother complex: Gregory (left) and Patrick (right) with Hemingway and Martha Gellhorn

Into these years falls the publication of *Death in the Afternoon* and *Green Hills of Africa*, both reports on a large scale. The former is an introduction to the bullfight, the latter describes a safari through the African bush, a hunting expedition for lions and elephants. The books had a divided reception. The colourful descriptions of scenery were generally admired, as were the complete mastery of the material and the exact rendering of every detail — *Death in the Afternoon* could pass as a manual for budding bullfighters. However, a number of critics took exception to Hemingway's scarcely concealed glorification of brute force. The book was considered bloodthirsty and objectionable. Edmund Wilson called it 'neurotic and hysterical'. Another critic, Lincoln Kirsten, wrote: 'For Hemingway, valor is almost the ability to die well, and his contempt for his fellows who accept an unheroic end is close to the snobbish contempt of a bully, without kindness, sympathy, and the profounder comprehension of the chemical roots of cowardice... Mr Hemingway believes in the courage of immediate physical action above all other. He is not busied with the courage of the mind, the energy of moral activity relentless in its penetration to the heart of the truth, unflinching at any self-imposed limits.'

The book had a peculiar sequel. Max Eastman, the American author who published an excellent Communist magazine during the First World War, made Lenin's Will public, wrote a noteworthy biography of Trotsky and is today among the most prominent fighters against Communism, attacked Hemingway with great bitterness. It was stupid, he said, to speak of a bull*fight,* for there was no fight. Men tortured and killed a bull, that was all. 'To drag in notions of honor and glory here, and take them seriously, is ungrown-up enough and rather sophomoric. But to pump words over it like tragedy and dramatic conflict is mere romantic nonsense and self-deception crying to heaven...'

Eastman went even further. He wondered why Hemingway should emphasise his virility to such a degree. 'Some circumstance seems to have laid upon Hemingway a continual sense of the obligation to put forth evidences of red-blooded masculinity. It must be made obvious not only in the swing of the big shoulders and the clothes he puts on, but in the stride of his prose style and the emotions he permits to come to the surface there. This trait of his character has been strong enough to form the nucleus of a new flavor in English literature, and it has moreover begotten a veritable school of fiction-writers, a literary style, you might say, of wearing false hair on the chest.'

This outburst rallied Hemingway's friends and followers to a counter-attack. Archibald MacLeish declared that Eastman had accused Hemingway of sexual impotence. Although Eastman replied that nothing had been further from his

The 'roof' of Africa: Mount Kilimanjaro

mind, the feud continued. It became a *cause célèbre* in the annals of American literature. The climax was reached four years later in a personal fight between Hemingway and Eastman when they happened to meet in Scribner's New York office.

The fight began when Hemingway tore open his shirt and proudly showed the bushy hair on his chest. Then he pulled open Eastman's shirt, showing that

Since his youth Hemingway's thoughts have centred on the Dark
Continent. Africa is his land of adventure. When, owing
to his successes, Hemingway became one of the wealthiest writers,
he was able to realise his dreams and go on safari

his chest was more sparsely covered. One word led to another and a few moments
later they came to blows. The reports of the two contestants about the course
and result of the affair differ considerably. Hemingway claimed to have 'disci-
plined' Eastman and presented a book with which he was alleged to have hit the
slanderer in the face; the blood-stain on one of the pages was supposed to be
the print of Eastman's nose. Eastman, on the other hand, declared that since
he was not endowed with Hemingway's talent for boxing, he had defeated him
by wrestling. The publishing staff who had appeared on the scene during the
fight refrained from making any statements about what they had witnessed and
merely confirmed that the office floor was littered with pens, pencils, files and
manuscripts, which they had to clear up.

Green Hills of Africa aroused less criticism, but neither did it inspire any
great admiration. Nevertheless, the adventures during this expedition provided
Hemingway with material for two short stories: *The Macomber Affair* and
The Snows of Kilimanjaro. These are among his best works. Quite justifiably,
they are considered equal to the classic stories of the great French and Russian
authors.

From his earliest childhood Africa held a particular fascination for Hemingway. As his biographer, Carlos Baker, stated, this interest was roused by the
novel *Batouala*, written by a Negro, René Maran, and honoured with the Prix
Goncourt. Hemingway discussed *Batouala* in 1922 in his first literary criticism.
Maran had conceived the novel as an accusation and protest against French
colonial policy. Hemingway, however, did not look into the political aspect, he
considered the book remarkable as a realistic description of life in an African
village. 'You smell the smells of the village', he wrote, 'you eat its food, you
see the white man as the black man sees him, and after you have lived in the

The Spanish Civil War: Madrid after an air-raid by Franco's air force

village you die there. That is all there is to the story, but when you have read it, you have been Batouala [the native chief], and that means that is a great novel.'

From then on Hemingway dreamed of making a trip to Africa and, above all, of hunting big game. The large income he received from his books enabled him to realise this dream in 1933.

The expedition lasted five months. He was afflicted with a painful attack of dysentery in the African bush and this necessitated a lengthy stay in a Nairobi hospital, but even this stroke of ill fortune he turned to his advantage. From it he gained inspiration and material for *The Snows of Kilimanjaro*.

The impressions and experiences he collected during his hunting trips provided him with the background for *The Macomber Affair*. Here again he ex-

In Barcelona: Republicans at the barricades

pounds the theme of courage and cowardice, but this time with a deeper, one might even say more human, understanding. The story is truly tragic because it is universally valid. Three people are the main characters of the drama: Francis Macomber, a rich American sportsman, his wife, Margot, and the guide accompanying them on their expedition, an Englishman by the name of Wilson.

Macomber is a weakling, completely dominated by Margot, who, cold and calculating, is a really terrifying representative of a certain type of American woman found in 'good society'. Fundamentally, the marriage is breaking, only outwardly held together by the fact that Margot is reluctant to part with her husband's wealth. She takes Wilson as her lover and does not even attempt to conceal the affaire, for she knows that her husband is too weak and cowardly to do anything about it. In addition she enjoys savouring her power over him, contemptuously proving it in this way. Macomber's weakness causes him great suffering. Twice he allows himself to look ridiculous in front of Wilson and the native bearers by running away from a wounded lion on the attack, and so loses even the last shreds of his self-respect.

However, this blow brings salvation. The next day he and Wilson track down a buffalo. The wounded animal suddenly attacks. This time Macomber does not turn to flee. Fearlessly he stares death in the face. He keeps on firing until the buffalo is only a few feet away and kills the animal. During these few minutes Macomber has found himself; at last a happy man, he has conquered his weakness. His happiness is short-lived, for Margot shoots him a few moments later. She begrudges Macomber the triumph of having proved himself as a man. He must die, as he threatens to escape from her domination.

The destructive power of wealth, the senseless greed for money and its pernicious effect on human relationships and on American life were subjects which occupied Hemingway to an ever-increasing extent during those years. The great economic crisis had aroused the social conscience of intellectual youth, artists and writers. It had shattered their faith in the capitalist economic system and turned them into Radicals. Many of them turned to Communism. Hemingway

Captured Franco officers: for them the bell had tolled

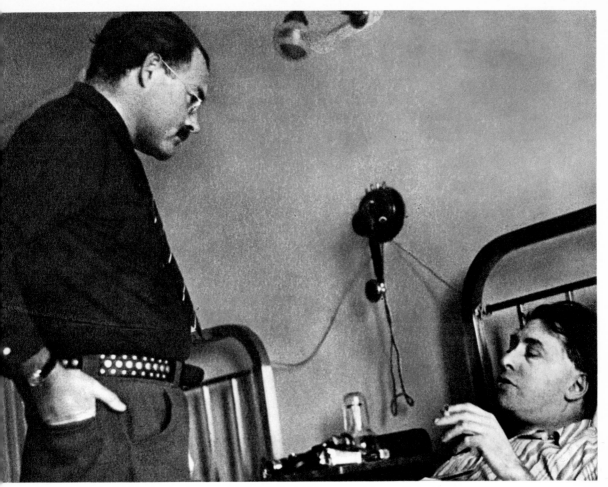
Co-existence among war correspondents: Hemingway and Ilya Ehrenburg outside Madrid

did not share their enthusiasm for the Communist ideology, but he too felt nothing but repugnance for the existing economic and social conditions. In *The Macomber Affair* he portrayed a marriage which he felt was typical of the decadence found in certain sections of rich American society. In these circles marriage had become a business, devoid of any sincere feeling and human warmth.

In *The Snows of Kilimanjaro* Harry, a writer dying of gangrene, sums up his life and concludes that in his quest for riches and luxury he has sacrificed art, love, freedom and intellectual independence. Memories of his youth, of Paris, float through his delirium. So many opportunities were open to him, he

The International Brigade: American passports, Spanish uniforms

had wanted to say so much of importance. The opportunities remained unused, he had let slip through his fingers everything that might have made his life worth living.

The same spirit of discontent dominates both stories; it also constitutes the focal point of Hemingway's next novel, *To Have and Have Not*.

Hemingway was caught up in the wave of social criticism. As the title of the book indicates it was to be a comparison between the world of the poor and that of the rich. However, Hemingway's attempt at a novel of social conditions was not successful. This was not because he was ignorant of these two worlds; he saw them both in Key West — the misery of the workless and the parasite existence of the rich and idle. He failed because he lacked one basic need of the social novelist: knowledge and understanding of the social and economic background of the times. His theory, which he puts into the mouth of the dying hero, Morgan, — whatever a man attempts, he can do nothing on his own — is not an inevitable result of the action, nor is it the fruit of intellectual development, but an adopted slogan. The character who puts it into words is a fisherman and a smuggler, the embodiment of an ideal, larger-than-life like the figures on Communist posters. It is characteristic of Hemingway's attitude that the poor man is a better lover than the gentleman, and his distinguished achievements in bed — in contrast to the sexual impotence of the perverted men of the world and society women — seem to provide the main proof of the supremacy of those who 'have not'.

There are thrilling episodes. When Hemingway describes the emptiness and intellectual poverty, especially with regard to sex, of the life of the 'haves' he achieves scenes which are among the most bitter and penetrating he has ever written. Thus he lets the wife of a popular writer scream all her disgust and horror of 'love' at her husband: 'Love was the greatest thing, wasn't it: . . . Slop.

The Civil War as novel and film: Gary Cooper and Ingrid Bergman (right) in *For Whom the Bell Tolls*. Both film and novel were banned in Spain

Love is just another dirty lie. Love is ergoapiol pills to make me come around.
. . . Love is quinine. . . . Love is that dirty aborting horror that you took me to.
Love is my insides all messed up. It's half catheters and half whirling douches.
I know about love. Love always hangs up behind the bathroom door. It smells
like lysol. . . . Love is all the dirty little tricks you taught me that you probably
got out of some book. All right. I'm through with you and I'm through with
love. Your kind of picknose love. You writer.'

Hemingway's fame was already on too firm a footing for the novel to be a
complete failure. Nevertheless, most of the critics attacked it more caustically
than is usual with such a well-known author. Only extreme left-wing factions
were full of admiration. They regarded Hemingway as a convert who had discovered his social conscience and would inevitably follow the path to the Communist Party. His courageous intercession in favour of the Spanish loyalists,
his vehement protest against Franco and his fascist allies seemed to confirm the
truth of the Communists' suppositions. They did not understand Hemingway's
true motives, the mental and spiritual impulses driving him.

Spain is Hemingway's great love. Africa represents temptation and adventure, Paris is an infatuation, Italy is Venice, a feast for the senses. Spain, though,
is the Spanish people. Hemingway has felt deeply involved with this people
ever since he first set foot in their country. The dignity of even the most simple
worker or farmer, the romantic individualism of the Spaniard — a mixture of
childish primitiveness, youthful exuberance and the resignation to suffering of
an ancient race, — but particularly the peculiar, almost mystical attitude of the
Spaniard towards death, which he respects with Catholic fervour and yet dis-
dains and even challenges with pagan delight — these contrasting elements were
particularly attractive to Hemingway and correspond to certain of his own.
This inner affinity also explains why Hemingway felt the tragedy of the Span-

Hemingway
at his
typewriter

'Finca Vigia',
Hemingway's home
in Cuba

ish freedom fighters far more deeply than the suffering and sacrifice of any other people under the yoke of Fascism.

When, in June 1937, he appeared on the platform at a congress of American writers in New York's Carnegie Hall and delivered his first — and to this day his last — political speech, he had just returned after two months at the Spanish front. The man who had so often declared that a writer's most important mission was to report objectively and refrain from taking sides, chose a side this time — clearly and vehemently. This did not mean, as many believed, that he wished to align himself with any political party or school. He made his position clear in his speech: 'Fascism is a lie told by bullies. A writer who will not lie cannot live and work under Fascism.' Hemingway was neither a Communist nor a socialist, he remained as he always had been — an anti-fascist.

Hemingway did not let matters rest with words and declarations of sympathy. In order to provide the Loyalists with much-needed medical supplies he personally raised 40,000 dollars and accepted the presidency of the committee of the 'American Friends of Spanish Democracy'. During the Civil War he travelled to Spain four times. He was always to be found where the fighting

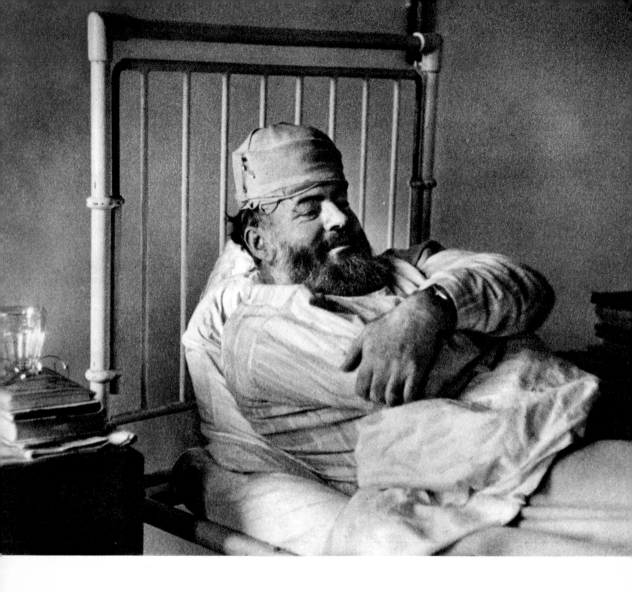

was at its height — in the trenches of the International Brigade and in besieged and starving Madrid. Together with the well-known Dutch film director, Joris Ivens, he made a documentary film, writing the commentary himself, an impassioned plea for the cause of the Spanish freedom fighters. At the request of President Roosevelt the first showing took place at the White House, then the film was shown all over the country and earned many thousands of dollars for the Spanish Aid Fund.

London, 1940: his 'umpteenth' accident

While in Madrid Hemingway wrote a play, *The Fifth Column*. His first, and so far his only, attempt at writing for the stage was unsuccessful. The drama was produced in New York, but Hemingway himself declared that it was probably his 'most unsatisfactory' work. While he was writing the play, the Florida Hotel where he was staying was hit by more than thirty bombs. He suggested that if the play were no good, this might well be the cause. The real reason, however, was entirely different. Carried away by his feelings, he had written a piece of pure propaganda, with all propaganda's typical deficiencies and superficiality.

Hemingway returned to his true medium when in March 1939 he began the draft of a novel using his impressions and experiences in Spain. *For Whom the Bell Tolls* became the crowning achievement of his literary career.

The book was attacked by Left and Right alike. The Communists protested against the representation of incompetence and confusion in the Loyalist camp. They took exception to the scenes showing the cruelty of the freedom fighters and the cold cynicism of the Soviet commissar. The party of the Right, on the other hand, treated with irony the acceptance of the revolution by the hero of the book, Robert Jordan, the American partisan, and accused Hemingway of being pro-Stalin. In truth the novel, in spite of its theme, is far from political. It reflects not only the rifts among the Spanish people, but also the confusion in Hemingway's mind. Because he is not a political writer, and is therefore unable to dedicate himself fully to any idea or ideology; because, tormented by doubts, he seeks a faith, yet mistrusts every faith, he experienced the Spanish Civil War as pure human tragedy. It revealed to him the futility of revolution, the betrayal of the Spanish people by the world powers — democracies and totalitarian states alike.

The main characters, representing the 'positive' elements — Jordan, the

During the Second World War: dedicated camp-follower to the Air Force

American, and Maria, the Spanish girl raped by the Fascists and freed from this horrible memory by her love for Jordan, — are not convincing. Their relationship is stereotyped, the uninhibited descriptions of their love-nights in the sleeping-bag often border on bad taste, giving the book a flavour of sensationalism. Hemingway's mastery asserts itself in the portrayal of the subsidiary characters, the local colour, the bloody fighting at the front and the intrigues in the background. These are the factors which ensure the novel its lasting place among the great works of world literature.

Hemingway took eighteen months to write this book. It was his greatest success, from a financial as well as a literary point of view. By December 1940, two months after publication, 200,000 copies had been sold, and by April 1941 the edition had topped the million mark. The film starring Ingrid Bergman as

– and at sea: the novelist on the bridge

Maria (Hemingway had sold the film rights only on condition that she and no other actress should play this part) contributed to the novel's extraordinarily wide circulation.

Hemingway was in Cuba in December 1941, when the Japanese Air Force attacked Pearl Harbour and America declared war on the Fascist powers. During the previous year he had acquired the estate of 'Finca Vigia' in San Francisco de Paula, a small fishing village eight miles from Havana, and there he lives the life of a gentleman-farmer. The spacious house is surrounded by gardens and lawns, a few cows provide the country atmosphere, innumerable cats, several dogs, doves and hens are favoured residents and their well-being is entrusted to the staff — a gardener, a cook, a maid and a chauffeur. The sitting room, 20 feet in length, displays the trophies of Hemingway's hunting

The invasion: from the port of Southampton to the coast of Normandy

expeditions. A tennis court and a swimming-pool provide the head of the house with the opportunity to indulge in his athletic activities. When he wishes to withdraw to his writing-table, he finds peace and solitude in the tower which houses his study. Hemingway's fishing ketch, *'Pilar'*, is anchored in the harbour, constantly ready to put to sea.

A few days after the publication of *For Whom the Bell Tolls* Pauline had won a divorce on the grounds of desertion, and shortly afterwards Hemingway married his third wife, Martha Gellhorn, the writer, again a girl from St Louis.

Hemingway was not going to miss this great event

They had got to know each other when she interviewed him for 'Colliers' magazine. Later, they met again in Spain, where she too was employed as a war correspondent.

This marriage only lasted four years. Hemingway's fourth wife, Mary Walsh, was a correspondent for the weekly magazine 'Time'.

It is extraordinary that not one of his four wives corresponded to the type of woman he idealised in his novels. All four were basically similar: 'career girls', highly intellectual and more than usually talented and successful in their

'Papa' Hemingway
and the soldiers (1944)

profession – in earlier times they would have been called blue stockings. No Lady Bratt and no Maria. As soon as Hemingway became divorced from one wife, he married, so to speak, her twin.

At the time Hemingway met Mary Walsh in London during the war he was assigned to the Royal Air Force as correspondent. In this capacity he repeatedly joined in sorties, winning great respect for his coolness and daring.

These flights were not his first contribution during World War II. Immediately after America's entry into the war, he volunteered with his fishing ketch. He had devised a strategy and the American ambassador in Cuba approved it. The boat was fitted with radio, machine guns and explosives, and was to serve as bait for German submarines. Should a U-boat challenge the ketch, Hemingway would feign surrender and then blow the U-boat out of the sea.

For two years Hemingway and his crew of nine sailed Cuba's coastal waters. The suicidal plan was never put into action, but several times Hemingway sighted enemy submarines which were subsequently sunk by the American fleet. The government rewarded his services with a medal for courage.

When the Allies landed in Normandy, Hemingway was assigned as reporter to the Infantry Division of the First American Army. He accompanied this

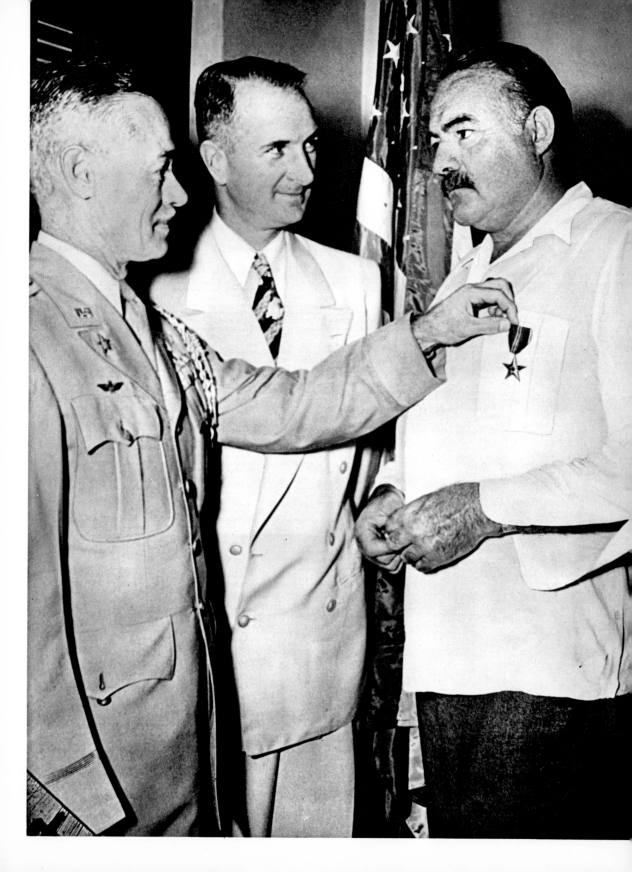

Hemingway was the faster:
he moved into Paris
before Leclerc (left)

Division during the advance on the Ardennes, always in the front line. The Division fought heavy and bloody battles, losing three-quarters of its officers and men in eighteen days.

When the spearhead of the American troops reached Rambouillet to the south-west of Paris and joined up with the Free French under General Leclerc to relieve Paris, Hemingway was in occupied territory fifty-five miles ahead of his troop. Here he once more tasted adventure. He assumed command of a group of French partisans and established headquarters in a farmhouse. He sent out patrols to ascertain the movements of the enemy forces. On Leclerc's arrival at the outpost Hemingway was able to present him with the results of his probings. Not satisfied with this, Hemingway and his 'army', now two thousand strong, joined Leclerc in the march on Paris. When Leclerc was held up by the Germans on the south bank of the Seine, Hemingway circumvented the enemy position and entered Paris at the head of his troop before Leclerc arrived. There was a small skirmish at the Arc de Triomphe, but by then the Allies had also entered the city and Hemingway accompanied the victors on their march along the Champs Elysées.

This piece of soldiering had an unexpected sequel for Hemingway. The Military Command instigated an official investigation into his activities, as he was under suspicion of having offended against the Geneva Convention, which emphatically stated that reporters were not allowed to carry arms. He was to appear before a court martial, but since so many witnesses testified that he personally had never carried arms, the proceedings were dropped. Instead of punishment, Hemingway received another medal for valour.

Almost eight years passed between the publication of *For Whom the Bell Tolls* and that of his next novel. The war was to blame for this long interruption in Hemingway's literary career.

Was it only the war? Or was Hemingway, perhaps, unwittingly providing

Hemingway in Venice, 1954

evidence for those critics who believed it to be a feature of American literature that the most gifted authors lost their creative talent while still comparatively young? Fame and wealth corrupted them. Hemingway had himself repeatedly dealt with this phenomenon, the dangers of American life for the serious author and artist. Had he become a victim of this same life?

When, at last, the novel *Across the River and into the Trees* was published, the critics' pessimism seemed to have been well-founded. Compared with Hemingway's earlier works the novel was undoubtedly a failure. The critics compared this story of a dying American colonel's last love affair in Venice with Thomas Mann's famous long short-story *Death in Venice*, and the comparison did not favour Hemingway. To compare the two, however, was misleading and unfair. *Death in Venice* is a brilliant psychological study of an ageing writer. The Venetian atmosphere, subtly suggesting decadence, envelops the story and gives it its particular charm. Hemingway's colonel is an embittered man, sick at heart, attempting to recapture his youth at the side of a young Italian countess. He and the girl are merely two-dimensional figures. The novel has no perspective – either intellectual, psychological or artistic.

Nevertheless, those who deduced from this unsuccessful book that Hemingway had 'written himself dry' were wrong, for two years later *The Old Man and the Sea* proved that his creative talent was still unimpaired. He had not sacrificed the high standard of artistic integrity he demanded of himself. The long short-story, certainly less complex and significant than his great novels, is of biblical simplicity. The language is so imaginative, the descriptions of nature so immediate, that one is reminded of Tolstoy's stories, for instance *The Snowstorm*. The relationship between the old fisherman and the young boy who admires and idolises him is touching.

It is true that the story lacks intellectual depth, but that is a limitation rooted in Hemingway's own being. It does not detract in any way from Hemingway's fanatically honest striving towards artistic perfection.

Hemingway's life has become rather more peaceful of late. Only twice has he

Spencer Tracy – the great 'old man'
in the film of Hemingway's fishing epic

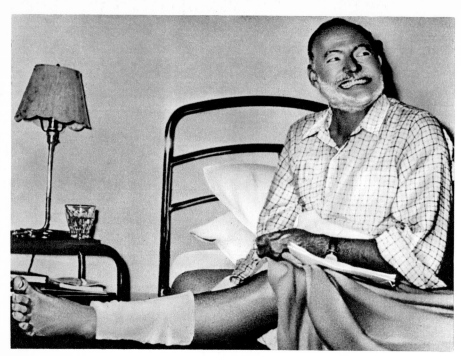

After the crash:
radio pictures
for the world's press
(1954)

achieved world headline status. In January 1954 he flew to Africa as a correspondent for the magazine 'Look' to report on the Mau-Mau territory. He
wanted to see Murchison Falls near the source of the White Nile and hired a
small aircraft, a single-engined Cessna. Shortly before the Falls the pilot, Roy
Marsh, was forced to alter course to avoid a flock of ibis, the aircraft dived
too low and made an emergency landing which severely damaged the under-
carriage. Hemingway suffered a slight head wound, his wife was uninjured.
There could be no thought of continuing the flight.

The Hemingways and the pilot decided to spend the night beside the aircraft.
As the author related, they had iron rations but no water, so they had to get this
from the Nile.

'The elephants didn't seem to like this and there were a number of cro-
codiles on the river bank who appeared to be decidedly annoyed,' Hemingway
said in a later interview. 'During the night an elephant prowled round our
camp for about two hours. Several times he was only twelve feet away. He
looked like a moving mountain in the moonlight. He seemed to listen most
attentively to my wife's loud snoring.

'When we woke her up, she said: "I never snore, that's just one of your ideas."
'I answered: "Obviously the elephant has the same idea."'

His rumbling laugh accompanied his wife's rather cross expression. Then he demonstrated to the reporters how he had howled like a wild dog during the night. All the other animals answered the howl, and he could tell where they were.

The next morning the Hemingways made their way to the Nile. A motor boat full of tourists soon appeared and took them to Butiabe on Lake Albert. Towards evening they embarked for Entebbe, the capital of Uganda, — again in a single-engined Cessna. This one crashed on take-off into a sisal plantation.

Reporters of all nationalities converged on East Africa. Hemingway: 'The news of my death is grossly exaggerated!'

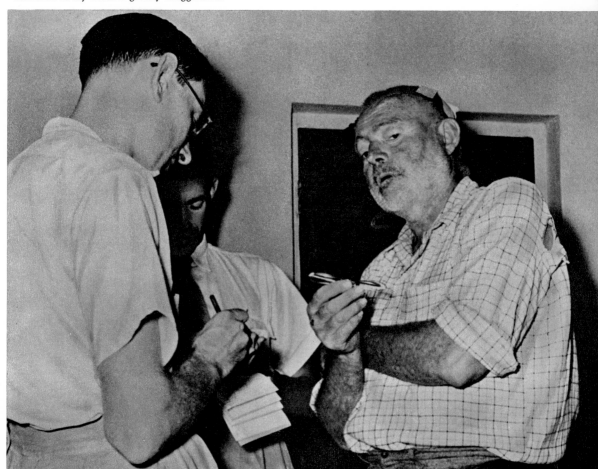

Seconds later it was a mass of flames. This time Mrs Hemingway was the sufferer. She broke two ribs. They finally reached Entebbe by police-car.

The award of the Nobel Prize of 1954 brought Hemingway's name into the limelight for the second time that year. The reason given by the Royal Swedish Academy for honouring him was that his power and skill had led to the creation of a new literary style, most recently embodied in *The Old Man and the Sea*. The prizewinner received 181,646 Swedish kroner (approximately £12,500). After Sinclair Lewis (1930), Eugene O'Neill (1936), Pearl S. Buck (1938) and William Faulkner (1949), Ernest Hemingway is the fifth American to be honoured by the Swedish Academy with the Nobel Prize for Literature.

A complaint brought against Hemingway shortly afterwards by a seventy-year-old Cuban fisherman, Miguel Ramirez, in connection with the filming of *The Old Man and the Sea,* was soon dismissed. The man claimed to have provided Hemingway with the material for his book and that in return the writer had promised him a motor boat and clothes. This accusation was so far-fetched, Hemingway's generosity in financial matters so widely known, that no one

Ernest Hemingway
– for once without beard

Gregory Hemingway
in the army

At home beneath
the palms:
Hemingway
in 'Finca Vigia'

In 'Finca Vigia':
war and revolution do
not penetrate here

could credit the fisherman's claim. It is more likely that this was a rumour spread by the film company for publicity reasons, since the film was ill-fated from the start. Costs were far greater than first estimated. The catching of the giant fish was to be screened in its entirety but no such fish could be found — weeks of expeditions and Hemingway's famed angling ability were unavailing. And in the end the film was not as financially successful as had been expected.

Since then 'Papa' and 'Miss Mary' — as they are called in Cuba — have lived in comparative seclusion. Hemingway's three sons often visit them. John,

In 'Finca Vigia':
Hemingway likes to listen
to the records of his friend,
Marlene Dietrich

Slide from a film:
memories of many
adventures

a man in his mid-thirties, won honours during the war. Patrick and Gregory have inherited their father's enthusiasm and talent for hunting and fishing.

In spite of his white beard, Hemingway is far from being a dignified patriarch. In outward appearance he is an old man, but this is really only a mask. Is it a

A glance through the window:
when is the next journey due?
Hemingway has not yet settled down.
He always has new plans –

conscious 'coquetry', the wish to be original that makes him appear a man older than his years? Or is it perhaps boyish high spirits, as if a twenty-year-old actor were anxious to shine in the role of a seventy-year-old?

For basically Hemingway is still young. He has preserved not only his youthful love of adventure, but also his continual striving to 'show off', to see himself admired, to dazzle his contemporaries. Nor have his honest temperament and refreshing ingenuousness diminished. Free of all self-conceit, but full of mistrust towards the 'arrogant and bloodless' intellectuals, he feels more at home among the fisherman and farmers of Cuba or Spain than in the literary circles of New York, a city he hates.

His youthfulness is Hemingway's particular charm. However, it also explains his artistic limitations. During four decades his work has gained nothing in

maturity and depth. He has not developed intellectually. 'A typical American', many European intellectuals will exclaim, and will put forward Hemingway's good and bad points as representing the character of the American people. They are wrong. America has changed greatly over the forty years since the Jazz Decade.

Faulkner, Thornton Wilder, and Thomas Wolfe belong to Hemingway's generation. What have they in common? Only one thing: loyalty to themselves; the uncompromising way in which each has pursued his own vision in the face of the temptations of wealth and power. And in the end, apart from genius or talent, it is the resolution with which an author keeps faith with himself, and the honesty with which he serves his art, which determine his position as a writer and importance as an artist.

Perhaps it will be a new novel

1899 21st July: Ernest Hemingway born in Oak Park, a small town in the state of Illinois.

1902 21st July: Hemingway's father gives him a fishing rod for his third birthday.

1909 At the age of ten Hemingway receives his first gun.

1917 Hemingway has finished school and is employed in Kansas City as local reporter for the 'Star'.

1918 April: Hemingway volunteers for military service in Europe as a member of the ambulance corps in the Italian army · July: Hemingway is seriously wounded and spends three months in hospital · October: Discharged as fit, he joins the Italian Infantry and is soon promoted to Lieutenant.

1919 January: Return to America.

1920 Journalistic work, first in Toronto on the 'Star Weekly' then in Chicago on the 'Chicago Tribune'.

1921 September: Marries Hadley Richardson. December: The young couple travel to Paris with a letter of introduction to Gertrude Stein.

1922 The friendship with Gertrude Stein and Ezra Pound provides him with inspiration and help in his serious writing. His assignments for the 'Star Weekly' take him from Paris to Germany, Italy, Switzerland and Greece.

1923 August: His first book, *Three Stories and Ten Poems,* is published in an edition of 300 copies by the Contact Publishing Company in Paris · October: Hemingway's first son, John, is born.

1924 His second book, *In Our Time,* is published in an edition of 170 copies by the Three Mountains Press, Paris. His first marriage is dissolved.

1926 Charles Scribner Sons, the New York publishers, issue the satirical short novel *Torrents of Spring* and secure the right to all further works by Hemingway. Marriage to Pauline Pfeiffer. *The Sun Also Rises* is published and achieves immediate success.

1927 Publication of the second volume of short stories, *Men Without Women.*

1928 Hemingway's second son, Patrick, is born. His father commits suicide.

1929 September: Publication of *A Farewell to Arms.* By the end of the year 80,000 copies have been sold.

1932 The third son, Gregory, is born. Publication of a book about bullfighting, *Death in the Afternoon.*

1933 A third volume of short stories, *Winner Take Nothing,* appears. *A Farewell to Arms* is filmed by Paramount. Hemingway undertakes a hunting expedition lasting five months through Africa.

1935 The travelogue *Green Hills of Africa* is published.

1936 Publication of the novel *To Have and Have Not.* As war correspondent in the Spanish Civil War, Hemingway supports the cause of the Spanish Republic.

1937 Hemingway's play about the Spanish Civil War, *The Fifth Column,* is printed but does not achieve success on the stage.

1939 March: Hemingway begins the draft of *For Whom the Bell Tolls.*

1940 Hemingway acquires the estate of 'Finca Vigia' in Cuba. His second marriage ends in divorce. Publication of *For Whom the Bell Tolls.*

1941 Marriage to Martha Gellhorn. The sales of *For Whom the Bell Tolls* pass the million mark.

1943 *For Whom the Bell Tolls* is filmed by Paramount with Ingrid Bergman and Gary Cooper in the leading roles.

1944 His third marriage ends in divorce. *To Have and Have Not* is filmed with Humphrey Bogart in the leading role (Warner Bros.). Marriage to Mary Walsh. He is war a correspondent at the French front.

1945 *The Killers,* one of Hemingway's short stories, is filmed by Universal, starring Ava Gardner and Burt Lancaster.

1947 *The Macomber Affair,* a United Artists film, starring Joan Bennett and Gregory Peck.

1949 Twentieth Century Fox adapt Hemingway's short story *My Old Man* to make the film *Under my Skin.*

1950 Publication of *Across the River and into the Trees. To Have and Have Not* is filmed a second time, again by Warner Bros., under the title *The Breaking Point.*

1952 Publication of *The Old Man and the Sea.* Twentieth Century Fox film *The Snows of Kilimanjaro,* with Susan Hayward, Ava Gardner and Gregory Peck in the leading roles · January: Commissioned by the magazine 'Look', Hemingway flies to Africa and is involved in two air crashes.

1954 December: Hemingway receives the Nobel Prize for Literature.

1957 *The Sun Also Rises* is filmed for the first time, *A Farewell to Arms* for the second, both by Twentieth Century Fox.

1958 Warner Bros. film *The Old Man and the Sea* with Spencer Tracy in the title role.

Frontispiece: ERNEST HEMINGWAY at his home near Havana in Cuba.
Photo, Malmberg

6 *To Have and Have Not.* This Hemingway novel was filmed in 1944 under the direction of Howard Hawks. William Faulkner wrote the script. The stars (left to right in the picture) were Lauren Bacall, Marcel Dalio, Humphrey Bogart. The film was made by Warner Bros.

7 DURING FILMING Hemingway discusses production with Spencer Tracy, the leading actor in *The Old Man and the Sea* (June, 1945). *Ullstein.*

8 MIGUEL LUIS DOMINGUIN, the famous Spanish bullfighter, visited Hemingway in Cuba in September 1954. *A.P.*

9 AT BULLFIGHTS in the Madrid bullring Hemingway studied the Matador's art.

10 MAIL from every corner of the world piles up on Hemingway's desk daily and reading it occupies much of his time, despite the help of a secretary. *Photo, Malmberg.*

12 DURING THE SPANISH CIVIL WAR Hemingway, whose sympathies were with Franco's opponents, spent several months in the front line trenches. *Photo, Robert Capa/Magnum.*

13 FISHING in the state of Idaho. Hemingway has won prizes in many countries for his angling and deep-sea fishing.

14/15 TROPHIES from Hemingway's various hunting expeditions in Africa are displayed on the walls of his living-room and study. *Photos, Malmberg.*

16 AFTER AN AIR CRASH in East Africa (1954) Hemingway describes the healing qualities of gin and whisky to reporters.

18 HEMINGWAY'S FATHER, Dr Clarence Edmonds Hemingway, was a successful doctor and dedicated huntsman. He was born in 1871 in Oak Park, committed suicide in 1928.

19 ERNEST AND MARCELLINE HEMINGWAY in an Oak Park High School yearly report. Beside the photographs the sporting and out-of-school activities are noted – a long list for both.

20 OAK PARK HIGH SCHOOL, the high school attended by Hemingway in his home town. Building alterations have since changed the appearance of the façade.

21 THE 'CLASS OFFICERS' in the Oak Park High School yearly report. Hemingway was prominent among them. *Archives.*

22 *The Trapeze*, the school magazine of Oak Park High School. Hemingway began his journalistic activity as a reporter for this paper.

23 SCHOOL SPORTS TEAMS, in three of which Hemingway was included: as a swimmer (top), as manager of the athletes (centre) and as a footballer (below). *Archives.*

24 THE SCHOOL MAGAZINE shows Hemingway's early journalistic career. At first Hemingway was just one of the reporters, but then he took over as editor. His sister, Marcelline, was one of his assistants. *Archives.*

25 RING LARDNER, an American novelist who drew his plots mainly from the world of sport, was so admired by Hemingway that the latter often published his articles for *The Trapeze* under Lardner's name. *Archives.*

26 'CLASS PROPHECY' was the annual attempt by one of the students to prophesy the future of his colleagues. Hemingway undertook this task in *Tabula*, the yearly report of Oak Park High School. *Archives.*

28 DURING THE FIRST WORLD WAR, the Austro-Hungarian army broke through the Italian positions on the River Isonzo in the autumn of 1917. The retreat was only halted at the Piave. *Ullstein.*

29 A 'WONDER WEAPON' of the First World War – the firing of an Austrian 30.5 cm. mortar at the Italian front.

31 *A Farewell to Arms*, Hemingway's great war novel, was filmed for the first time in 1933 under the direction of Frank Borzage, and starred Gary Cooper, Helen Hayes and Adolphe Menjou.

32 HEMINGWAY IN HOSPITAL in Milan after he had been seriously wounded.

33 WAR EXPERIENCE on film: Gary Cooper and Helen Hayes in *A Farewell to Arms*, first filmed in 1933.

The Sun Also Rises, starring Tyrone Power and Ava Gardner, filmed in 1957 by Twentieth Century Fox.

35 HEMINGWAY'S PARENTS' HOUSE in Oak Park, Kenilworth 600, near Chicago.

36 FROM 1920 TO 1924 – with several interruptions – Hemingway worked as a reporter on the 'Toronto Star'. *Archives.*

37 CHICAGO. Hemingway lived here in 1920 and 1921, before taking over as European correspondent for the 'Toronto Star'. *Keystone.*

38 AUTHORS Hemingway admired: Mark Twain (1835–1910), Henry James (1879–1947), William Butler Yeats (1865–1939).

40 SHERWOOD ANDERSON (1876–1941), founder of the so-called 'Chicago school', exerted an important influence on American literature after the First World War. *Ullstein.*

41 WILLIAM FAULKNER (born 1897) was a pilot in the Royal Air Force during the First World War. The portrait was painted by his mother, Maud Faulkner. *Ullstein.*

43 'THE TORONTO STAR WEEKLY' published many of Hemingway's reports from Europe and the Near East during the early 'twenties. One of correspondent Hemingway's favourite subjects was bullfighting. *'Toronto Star Weekly', Archives.*

44 THE 'MOULIN ROUGE' in Paris, the famous night-club at the beginning of the 'twenties. *Ullstein.*

45 GERTRUDE STEIN (1874–1946), born in America, lived in Paris from 1903 onwards with her friend and secretary, Alice B. Toklas. In possession of a large fortune, she used her wealth to encourage young artists of the modern school, among them Picasso, Matisse and Braque. When Hemingway arrived in Paris they took to

each other. She 'discovered' him and encouraged his first literary attempts. After a sculpture by Joe Davidson. *Photo, Ullstein.*

46 THE CAFE DE LA PAIX on the Boulevard des Capucines in Paris during the 'twenties. *Ullstein.*

47 EZRA POUND (born 1885), like Gertrude Stein, encouraged Hemingway's early literary efforts. *Ullstein.*

48 JAMES JOYCE (1882–1941) was a member of the literary circle joined by Hemingway in Paris. *Photo, Gisèle Freund.*

49 FRANCIS SCOTT KEY FITZGERALD (1896 –1940) was considered a prodigy of American literature during the 'twenties and 'thirties. Through him Hemingway got his first publishing contract in Paris in 1923. *U.S.I.S.*

50 BENITO MUSSOLINI during the march on Rome (28th October, 1922). From left to right in the picture: Italo Balbo, General de Bono, Mussolini. *Ullstein.*

51 GIACOMO MATTEOTTI, leader of the Italian Socialists, was murdered on Mussolini's orders on 10th June, 1924.

52 THE GENOA CONFERENCE (April 1922): reporters mob the British Prime Minister, Lloyd George, as he leaves the Conference building. *Ullstein.*

53 THE GENOA CONFERENCE, 1922: Lloyd George (second from left) in conversation with the French Foreign Minister, Barthou (fourth from left). *Ullstein.*

54 THE OCCUPATION OF THE RUHR (1923) by France led to Separationist demonstrations, which were supported by the occupational forces. Here a leader of the Separationists makes a speech in Krefeld (1923). *Ullstein.*

55 FRENCH TROOPS entering the Ruhr in 1923. *Ullstein.*

56 STREET SCENE in the occupied Ruhr area (1923). *Ullstein.*

57 IN THE OCCUPIED RUHR: French armoured cars in front of the main station in Essen (1923). *Ullstein.*

58 THE GRAECO-TURKISH WAR began in 1919 with the landing of Greek troops in Smyrna. Retribution came in 1922 when Kemal Pasha drove the Greeks out of Asia Minor. *Ullstein.*

60 IVAN TURGENEV (1818–1883), whom Hemingway greatly revered. *Handke.*

61 HEMINGWAY AS A BULLFIGHTER. In the summer of 1924, accompanied by his first wife, he took part in a fiesta in Pamplona. He ventured into the bullring and was slightly injured by one of the bulls; his friend, Donald Ogden Stewart, who had gone with him, was carried off with several broken ribs. Report in the 'Toronto Star' of 30th July, 1924. *Archives.*

62 COUNT LEO TOLSTOY (1828–1910) was in Hemingway's view too 'philosophical'. Nevertheless he modelled much of his work on Tolstoy's. *Ullstein.*

63 *In Our Time*, the title page of the edition which appeared in Paris in 1924. This collection of short stories was the second of Hemingway's books to be published.

64 MUSTAPHA KEMAL PASHA (called Atatürk), founder of modern Turkey, which came into being at the Conference of Lausanne in 1923, with the end of the Graeco-Turkish conflict.

Hemingway was present at the Conference as a reporter. *Ullstein.*

65 Kemal Atatürk among farmers during the Graeco-Turkish war.

66 SYLVIA BEACH, an American girl living in Paris, provided a literary centre for the American expatriates with her book-shop 'Shakespeare and Co.' *Photo, Gisèle Freund.*

67 ARCHIBALD MACLEISH (born 1892), the American poet, was one of Hemingway's closest friends during his years in Paris. *U.S.I.S.*

68/69 AT 'SHAKESPEARE & Co.': James Joyce with Sylvia Beach, who published *Ulysses* after it had been banned in England and America. *Photo, Gisèle Freund.*

70 ROBERT MCALMON was Hemingway's first publisher (at the Contact Publishing Company). In 1923 he published a selection of Hemingway's poems and short stories under the title *Three Stories and Ten Poems* in an edition consisting of 300 copies.

71 EZRA POUND'S STUDIO in Paris, a meeting place for the Bohemians during the 'twenties.

GERTRUDE STEIN in her studio in Paris: Hemingway was a frequent visitor.

72 HEMINGWAY AND SYLVIA BEACH in front of the book-shop 'Shakespeare and Co.' in Paris.

73 ERNEST HEMINGWAY, a portrait study by Man Ray, who later became famous as an abstract painter.

74 HEMINGWAY'S HANDWRITING — the address on a letter sent to Sylvia Beach.

75 ERNEST HEMINGWAY towards the end of the 'twenties, after his return to America.

77 AFTER HIS FIRST SUCCESSES: Hemingway continually supplied new topics for gossip — in the role of huntsman, angler, boxer, bullfighter. He had no further need to worry about publicity. *Archives.*

78 *A Farewell to Arms*, the first film version of a Hemingway novel, was made in 1933, directed by Frank Borzage for Paramount. The film was a huge success; a second adaptation was screened in 1957 under the direction of Charles Vidor, a Selznick production for Twentieth Century Fox. The leading roles were played by Tyrone Power and Ava Gardner.

79 *The Sun Also Rises*, Hemingway's first great novel (1926), was not filmed until 1957 because of possible censorship difficulties. Henry King directed it, Tyrone Power and Ava Gardner were the stars. (Zanuck/Twentieth Century Fox).

80 *To Have and Have Not* was filmed in 1944. It was directed by Howard for Warner Bros.

81 THE FILM *The Killers*, starring Burt Lancaster and Ava Gardner, was adapted in 1945, under the direction of Robert Siodmak, from Hemingway's short story of the same name. (Universal).

82/83 *The Snows of Kilimanjaro*, a film adapted from Hemingway's short story of the same name. Directed by Henry King (1952, Zanuck/Twentieth Century Fox). The leading roles were played by Gregory Peck, Susan Hayward, Ava Gardner and Hildegard Knef.

85 HEMINGWAY'S HOUSE in Key West on the southern tip of Florida, bought after his first great success. *A.P.*

86 HEMINGWAY'S SECOND MARRIAGE. In 1928 Hemingway married his second wife Pauline Pfeiffer. They were divorced in 1940. There were two sons of this marriage, Gregory and Patrick. *U.P.I.*

87 HEMINGWAY'S THIRD MARRIAGE lasted four years. In 1940 he married the writer,

Martha Gellhorn; in 1941 they were divorced. *U.I.P.*

HEMINGWAY AND MARY WALSH, his fourth wife, were married in 1944 in London during the Second World War.

88 A FAVOURITE HUNTING EXPEDITION to Sun Valley: Hemingway with his sons, Gregory and Patrick, and Mrs Gary Cooper. *Robert Capa/Magnum.*

89 GREGORY AND PATRICK, the sons of Hemingway's second marriage, were still welcomed at their father's home after he had remarried. They were on good terms with all their step-mothers (in the picture: Martha Gellhorn). *Capa/Magnum.*

91 HEMINGWAY'S 'MOUNTAIN OF DESIRE', Mount Kilimanjaro in East Africa. Many of his short stories are set in this countryside, through which he often travelled. *Ullstein.*

92 LANDSCAPE IN KENYA, the East African hunting paradise. *Ullstein.*

94 THE SPANISH CIVIL WAR. In the streets of Madrid after an air-raid by the Nationalists in 1936. As a dedicated anti-fascist, Hemingway supported the Republicans. *Ullstein.*

95 THE SPANISH CIVIL WAR. Republicans behind the paving-stone barricades they had set up in Barcelona (1936). *Ullstein.*

96 OFFICERS OF FRANCO'S ARMY captured in Madrid are led away by Republicans. *Ullstein.*

97 HEMINGWAY IN SPAIN. The American war correspondent with the Russian star reporter, Ilya Ehrenburg, at the Madrid front. *Robert Capa/Magnum.*

98 THE INTERNATIONAL BRIGADE: the 'Abraham Lincoln Batallion', consisting of American volunteers, defended the University quarter of Madrid; during the heavy fighting even books were used for the barricades. Hemingway spend several days with his American comrades in their positions. *Robert Capa/Magnum.*

99 *For Whom the Bell Tolls* was Hemingway's greatest success. The film – starring Gary Cooper and Ingrid Bergman – was also a world-wide triumph. (Direction: Sam Wood, 1943; Paramount).

100 GARY COOPER AND INGRID BERGMAN in the film *For Whom the Bell Tolls.* Hemingway gave his permission for the making of the film only on condition that Ingrid Bergman played Maria. *U.S.I.S.*

102 'FINCA VIGIA' Hemingway's estate in Cuba, is situated thirty miles outside Havana. Bought during the Second World War, the property has become his favourite home. *U.S.I.S.*

103 HEMINGWAY often writes standing up. He writes narrative passages in pencil but uses the typewriter for dialogue.

104 AFTER A CAR CRASH in London, which was being bombed by the Germans at the time, Hemingway had to spend several weeks in an English hospital (1940).

106 DURING THE SECOND WORLD WAR Hemingway acted as a war correspondent apart from a short period on active service in Cuban waters. The picture shows him before a reconnaissance flight in England in 1944. *A.P.*

107 BEFORE THE INVASION: Hemingway on board a ship of the U.S. Navy before the start of the landings on the French coast.

108 THE INVASION, 1944; thousands of landing craft in Southampton harbour on the eve of the landings. *Ullstein.*

Notes on the plates

109 ALLIED TROOPS during the landings on the Normandy beaches (6th June, 1944). *Ullstein.*

110 HEMINGWAY AS WAR CORRESPONDENT with British soldiers during the invasion. *A.P.*

111 THE 'BRONZE STAR' for valour was awarded to Hemingway for his services during World War II. He received the medal in Cuba from Colonel Edgar E. Glenn in the presence of the U.S. Ambassador, L. D. Mallory (centre).

112 MARSHAL LECLERC, the Commander of the Free French was the first Allied General to reach Paris. Hemingway had joined his force. *D.P.A.*

113 HEMINGWAY IN VENICE: He loves this city and used it as background for his novel *Across the River and into the Trees* (March 1954). *Keystone.*

115 *The Old Man and the Sea,* the great work of Hemingway's old age, was filmed in 1958. John Sturges directed it, and the title role was played by Spencer Tracy. (Warner Bros.)

116 ACCIDENT IN KENYA: In January 1954, Hemingway suffered various injuries in two air crashes in East Africa. The news caused a sensation in the world's press. *U.P.I.*

117 AN INTERVIEW after the accident in East Africa: Hemingway reports in detail on his most recent adventure. *U.P.I.*

118 GREGORY HEMINGWAY, the author's second son, joined the U.S. Parachute troops in 1956. *U.P.I.*

119 ERNEST HEMINGWAY, a portrait study by George Rodgers.

120/21 IN THE GARDEN of 'Finca Vigia': the writer takes a walk. *Malmberg.*

122/23 AT 'FINCA VIGIA': Hemingway at home. *Malmberg.*

124 FAVOURITE RECORDINGS are songs by Marlene Dietrich. *Malmberg.*

125 THE EXTENSIVE LIBRARY at 'Finca Vigia'. *Malmberg.*

126/27 HEMINGWAY at the window at 'Finca Vigia'. *Malmberg.*

128 IN HIS ROOM, Hemingway at 'Finca Vigia'. *Malmberg.*

The works of Ernest Hemingway are published in Great Britain by Jonathan Cape Limited and in the United States of America by Charles Scribner and Company.

INDEX OF NAMES

Numbers in italics refer to the illustrations